A NOBLE AND POTENT LADY

Katherine Campbell, Countess of Crawford
(d. 1578)

Mary Verschuur

Number 46
Dundee
2006

ISBN 0 900019 43 3

Printed by Tayport Printers
Tel: (01382) 552381

CONTENTS

LIST OF ABBREVIATIONS

ADCS — The Acts and Decreets of the Lords of Council and Session (NAS).

CSPS — *Calendar of State Papers Relating to Scotland and Mary Queen of Scots, 1547-1603*, ed. J. Bain (Edinburgh, 1889-1969).

Crawford Muniments — Muniments of the Earl of Crawford and Balcarres containing the papers of Catherine Lindsay (neé Campbell), Countess of Crawford, wife of the ninth earl, NLS Accession 9769.

The Haigh Inventory — 'Inventory of Scottish Muniments at Haigh.' A detailed typescript list of Scottish deeds and other papers undertaken by the NRA(S) in 1920 and now housed with the Crawford Muniments in the NLS, Accession 9769.

IR — *The Innes Review.*

NAS — The National Archives of Scotland.

NLS — The National Library of Scotland.

RD — The Register of Deeds (NAS).

RMS — *The Register of the Great Seal of Scotland*, ed. J.M. Thompson and others (Edinburgh, 1882-1914).

RPC — *The Register of the Privy Council of Scotland*, ed. J.H. Burton and D. Masson (Edinburgh, 1877-98).

RSS — *Registrum Secreti Sigilli Regum Scotorum*, ed. M. Livingstone and others (Edinburgh, 1908-82).

Scots Peerage — *The Scots Peerage*, ed. Sir James Balfour Paul (Edinburgh 1904-14).

SHR — *The Scottish Historical Review.*

SHS — Scottish History Society.

LIST OF ILLUSTRATIONS

LIST OF TABLES

GLOSSARY OF SCOTS WORDS

Proper names that are frequently spelt in different ways in the sources, even on the same page, have been standardised throughout.

All dates are given according to the new style i.e. beginning the year on 1 January.

Sums of money are given in pounds Scots or in 'merks', one merk being worth two thirds of one pound.

The prefix 'sir' (lower case) refers to a cleric. 'Mr' refers to a person qualified as a Master of Arts.

Bairn: a child, offspring.

Decreet: a final judgment (in law).

Feu: a payment or rent to a superior for heritable possession of a piece of land.

Fiar: the owner of the fee-simple of a property.

Geir: possessions.

Moveables: property which is not heritable such as personal belongings, jewellery, etc.

Poind: seize and sell the goods of a debtor.

Tack: a lease, especially the leasehold tenure of a farm.

Tailze: the settlement of heritable property on a specified line of heirs (in law).

Terce: the right of a widow to the liferent of one third of her husband's heritable estate (in law).

Teind: a tenth part, usually referring to the tenth part of the produce of a parish for the support of religion.

Tocher: a bride's dowry.

Wadset: a mortgage of property, with conditional right of redemption.

PREFACE

I met Katherine Campbell quite by accident in the summer of 2000 when I was asked if I might like to fill in some gaps in *The Oxford DNB* which was then a work in progress. Katherine was the only female person on the list offered to me and I thought that she might be a most interesting subject. I must admit that I knew nothing about her at the time, but what began as a 600-word biography of one remarkable sixteenth-century countess of Crawford sparked my interest and motivated me to find out more about this noble and potent lady who was frequently addressed by this appellation in both her legal and personal papers.

The research for this work would have been impossible without the kind assent of The earl of Crawford and Balcarres. He generously granted me permission on more than one occasion to access the Personal Papers of Katherine Lindsay, neé Campbell, and other documents relevant to her life and affairs, on deposit amongst the Muniments of the Earl of Crawford and Balcarres in the National Library of Scotland (Accession 9769). He also provided the photographs of her prayer book. Likewise the assistance of Kenneth Dunn, senior curator at the NLS, was invaluable in expediting delivery of the papers during my visits to Scotland. I must acknowledge his generosity in giving of his time and support both while I was at the NLS and in making the necessary arrangements for my visits. Angus Council's Cultural Services also kindly gave permission for the reproduction of the nineteenth-century illustration of Edzell Castle.

A travel grant from the Charles and Mary Caldwell Martin Fund, administered by the Department of History at the University of Nebraska at Omaha, partially supported my first visit to the NLS. Mrs Honor Reid drove me all over Angus and Forfar seeking out many of the places associated with the life of the countess and when the work was coming to fruition and required a detached critique, Maureen Meikle kindly took it upon herself to read the manuscript draft for me. Her comments and suggestions were both helpful and insightful, and her proposals for further reading on my part were invaluable in broadening my perspective. Like debts of gratitude go to my editor Dr Alan MacDonald for his perceptive reading and shared insights, to Matthew Jarron who guided the book through the printing and final proof-reading process and to the Abertay Historical Society in general for selecting this subject for its annual publication.

We bring to our study of the past a desire to present the truth but this is frequently clouded by our own prejudices and interpretations. As I drove up the glens of Angus or walked on the beach at Lunan Bay looking up at Redcastle, I often asked myself, 'Did Katherine Campbell ever walk or ride here? Did she enjoy the many moods of the glens and valleys or the sweeping curve of sand, backed by the high dunes?' I have not discovered any reference to her love of her surroundings so these questions must, of course, remain unanswered, but I did grow to like and admire my subject very much as I learned more and more about her from her letters and papers. Consequently, if I have crossed the lines between historical fact and personal prejudice I ask you, the reader of this work, for your indulgence. If I have allowed my prejudice and admiration to cause me to have misrepresented Katherine Campbell in any way, this and any ensuing errors are my failings.

I am sure that although I have brought Katherine Campbell out of the shadows, there is a great deal more to be discovered about her. I am equally sure that without the help and cooperation of all of those mentioned above, Katherine Campbell might still be hidden in the archives.

Omaha, Nebraska   April 2006

INTRODUCTION

The pervasive presence of women in the sixteenth century is constantly proclaimed, despite the fact that they do not appear as frequently as men either in positions of power or in the records. We catch glimpses of them when they come into view as wives and daughters of particular men. Their marriage contracts tell us to whom they were married and on what terms. Their testaments reveal family relationships and household arrangements while legal papers and processes indicate a wide range of actions and affairs into which women might be drawn, and of which, occasionally, they took direction. Yet, beyond these formal instruments we have few clues as to who a particular woman really was, how she was educated, how she thought or felt, or of how she expressed her emotions or her sympathies. Most of that remains hidden behind such phrases as 'the wife of' or 'for her interest'.

Scottish women from all eras are currently undergoing a renaissance as historians look more carefully at their appearances in public and private record collections. A *Biographical Dictionary of Scottish Women*[1] published in March 2006 offers readers and researchers a useful tool in their work. Elizabeth Ewan and Maureen Meikle have brought together an extensive collection of essays in *Women in Scotland c.1100-c.1750*.[2] Numerous contributors explore briefly but succinctly some of the many roles filled by early modern women from all walks of life with substantial coverage given to sixteenth-century women. The overall opening up of that theme is powerful.

Yet another detailed and personally revealing work on sixteenth-century Scottish women, their lives, cares and skills, are the sections dedicated to the female experience in Margaret Sanderson's *A Kindly Place?*[3] Two chapters in particular, one describing women's status and subsistence, and another on women's handwriting are derived from the author's 'longstanding interest in women's history'.[4] Each is replete with details about the lives of ordinary women, unmarried,

married and widowed, who belonged to widely different social groups and who performed a broad range of social, cultural and professional services.

A third, informative portrait of a remarkable Scottish woman is to be found in Jane Dawson's *Clan Campbell Letters*.[5] Although not dedicated to women's letters and writing per se, Dr Dawson's collection discloses a prodigious store of information about Campbell women as revealed through their correspondence with others as well as from the letters written to the Campbell ladies by spouses, statesmen and family members. Of particular note are the letters of Katherine Ruthven, wife of Colin Campbell of Glenorchy, who was a prolific letter-writer. In correspondence with her husband and his political colleagues, or in communications to her kin and friends, Katherine Ruthven exposes the important role played by sixteenth-century noblewomen whose contributions to family life and family strategies have to date 'been seriously underestimated'.[6]

Officially, sixteenth-century women were inferior in status and in law. Although single women over 21 years of age or widows might enjoy a certain degree of freedom or the power to exercise some independent action, a wife had few legal rights since on marriage she and all her affairs and possessions (with the exception of her clothing and jewellery) came under the management and direction of her husband. One slight protection was offered to her in that the liferent lands normally bestowed upon a wife at the time of her marriage could not be alienated by her spouse without her consent.[7] On the other hand, a wife could not act in any way without her husband's permission.[8] Any freedom she might enjoy was highly dependent on the goodwill of her spouse, although some who have looked closely at this issue have concluded that 'many wives …. were not as legally constrained as theory might suggest'.[9]

There is general agreement that the greatest degree of female independence was achieved by widows, so long as they did not re-marry.[10] A widow's financial independence was guaranteed in her terce rights, which provided her with a place to live as well as rents and other incomes from land. Moveables and other land might offer further income and could be rented out or otherwise invested by her as long as a widow remained unmarried.[11] Noble women had an advantage in usually having more expendable income of these sorts with which to work.

Then too, widows were frequently given custody of their children and were free to act in court on behalf of these children, as they did often. They could bring suits to court personally or through a procurator and in general had 'more freedom of action than wives in legal and financial affairs'.[12] Arranging the marriages of her children was another way in which a widow might exercise some control. Janet Hepburn, whose husband, George fifth Lord Seton, was killed at Flodden, managed family affairs and arranged marriages for her daughters, even after entering the convent of Sciennes.[13]

The subject of this book, Katherine Campbell, countess of Crawford (d. 1578) was one of those aristocratic Scottish women who personified many of the traits identified above. She began her married life as the wife of James, master of Ogilvy and was identified 'for her interest' in the few documents relating to their marriage. Briefly widowed, she engaged in some independent actions, only to be remarried and thus to come under the jurisdiction of her second husband, David, ninth earl of Crawford. While married to him, Katherine seems to have enjoyed his trust and goodwill and she was able to exercise her independence, even if legally she required his consent to do so. Following the earl's death Katherine became a widow for the second time and in the twenty years thereafter she was not required to marry yet again. She was thus able to enjoy and to engage actively in all of the pursuits, financial, legal and parental, which opened up to her as a widowed woman of means.

This is her story. I will write of her as Katherine Campbell since she almost always signed her name Katherine Campbell or countess of Crawford. Married Scots women, unlike their English counterparts, retained their own surnames and although Katherine appears formally as Katherine Lindsay née Campbell in the Index to the Crawford Muniments, I will use her own name throughout.[14] I might offer as support for my decision to do this the example of Jane Dawson who cites Katherine, wife of Colin Campbell of Glenorchy as Katherine Ruthven.[15]

NOTES

[1]   *The Biographical Dictionary of Scottish Women*, ed., E. Ewan and others (Edinburgh, 2006).

[2]   E. Ewan and M. Meikle, eds., *Women In Scotland c.1100 - c.1750* (East Linton, 1999).

[3]   M. Sanderson, *A Kindly Place? Life in Sixteenth-Century Scotland* (East Linton, 2002), esp. chs. 8 and 9.

[4]   *Ibid.*, Introduction, viii. The theme of women in Scotland is addressed from a different perspective by Y. Brown and R. Ferguson, eds., *Twisted Sisters: Crime and Deviance in Scotland Since 1400* (East Linton, 2002).

[5]   *Clan Campbell Letters 1559-1583*, ed. J. Dawson (SHS, 1997).

[6]   *Ibid.*, 34, 22-34. Dawson also discusses the contents of some of Katherine Ruthven's letters and assesses the role she played in family affairs. A valuable resource for comparisons with the lives of aristocratic Englishwomen is B. Harris, *English Aristocratic Women 1450-1550. Marriage and Family, Property and Careers* (Oxford, 2002).

[7]   R. Reddington-Wilde, 'A Woman's Place: Birth Order, Gender and Social Status in Highland Houses', in *Women in Scotland*, ed. Ewan and Meikle, 207.

[8]   Sanderson, *Kindly Place?*, 99; W. Coutts 'Wife and Widow: The evidence of Testaments and Marriage Contracts c. 1600', in *Women in Scotland*, ed. Ewan and Meikle, 176-7.

[9]   *Ibid.*, 176, 179, 184; Sanderson, *Kindly Place?*, 99, 133; J. Finlay, 'Women and Legal Representation in Early Sixteenth-Century Scotland', in *Women in Scotland*, ed. Ewan and Meikle, 166.

[10] *Ibid.*, 167 cites the example of Margaret Tudor widow of King James IV; Coutts, 'Wife and Widow', 178.

[11] Sanderson, *Kindly Place?*, 116-23; Coutts, 'Wife and Widow', 179.

[12] Finlay, 'Women and Legal Representation', 169; Sanderson, *Kindly Place?*, 116.

[13] J. P. Foggie, *Renaissance Religion in Urban Scotland The Dominican Order, 1450-1560* (Leiden, 2003), 79.

[14] NLS, The Crawford Muniments, Acc. 9769; *The Oxford Dictionary of National Biography*, ed. H. Matthews and others (Oxford, 2004), lists her under the surname Campbell.

[15] *Campbell Letters*, ed. Dawson, 290 (Index).

1

KATHERINE CAMPBELL
MISTRESS OF OGILVY

In the early sixteenth century, Angus was not one of those parts of Scotland normally associated with Campbell dominance. In fact, it was a region where a Campbell presence was limited and its influence negligible. By the middle of the century this situation had been altered markedly by what Ted Cowan has referred to as the 'planting of a kindred'.[1] The earls of Argyll as chiefs of clan Campbell had adopted a policy, early on, of extending their influence through propitious marriages into families in areas adjacent to and beyond their immediate highland base.[2] This practice had been begun in Angus when in 1526 Donald Campbell, youngest son of the second earl of Argyll, was 'planted' in the area. With a little help from James V and others (notably Cardinal Wolsey), Campbell won appointment to the influential ecclesiastical office of abbot of the Cistercian abbey of Coupar Angus.[3] He later sought other offices, including nomination to the bishoprics of Dunkeld, Glasgow and Brechin, but he was unsuccessful in these quests though he remained titular abbot of Coupar Angus until his death in 1562.[4] In his lifetime he fathered numerous children to whom he provided land and income out of the abbey's estates. His generosity caused one expert on feuing to note 'it is surprising that, given the circumstances of the late 1550s, the whole of the Coupar Angus estates did not pass into the hands of the aged abbot's relatives, cadet branches of the powerful house of Argyll.'[5]

Another Campbell, John, an illegitimate son of the first earl, began to acquire property in Angus at about the same time. John Campbell entered the service of the king from whom he received gifts and grants of land in Angus. Not only that, but John married a daughter of the second Lord Gray, sheriff of Forfar, who brought to the marriage the lands of Lundie and to her husband the title of John

Campbell of Lundie.[6]

Women too played important roles in the expansion and maintenance of Campbell influence. The third Campbell to 'occupy' Angus in the first half of the sixteenth century was Katherine, daughter of John Campbell of Calder (Abbot Donald's brother) and Muriel, heiress of Cawdor. As was so often the case amongst noble families, a marriage strengthened the affinity and was generally arranged to bring about a union of families rather than of individuals.[7] Katherine's two marriages, first to James master of Ogilvy, and, following his death at Pinkie in 1547, to David Lindsay of Edzell, ninth earl of Crawford, placed her into the heart of both the leading families in Angus society.[8] If 'Clan Campbell's primary concern was to acquire power over an area, not merely to occupy land' the appointment of Abbot Donald and the marriages arranged for Katherine Campbell offer proof of clan policy.[9]

The society into which Katherine Campbell was introduced through marriage was one in which social contacts and connections amongst families formed a 'labyrinthine' network of relationships and landholding.[10] It was an intricate and localized society in which even the most influential lords had insufficient power and wealth to hold sway independently and it was made more complex by intermarriage amongst the leading families. To cite but a few examples, James third Lord Ogilvy was married to the daughter of the seventh earl of Crawford and sister to the eighth earl. The fourth Lord Ogilvy and Alexander, master of Crawford each married one of the daughters of Henry, third Lord Sinclair. The fourth Lord Ogilvy's many daughters all married into local families forging connections between Ogilvy and Innermeath, Gray, Graham of Fintry and Erskine of Brechin.[11] John Erskine of Dun, who later became a close associate of the ninth earl of Crawford and Katherine Campbell, was married briefly to Elizabeth, a daughter of the eighth earl of Crawford.[12] Katherine's marriage into the family of Ogilvy definitely digresses from this pattern, she being brought in from outside the region to wed the fourth Lord Ogilvy's son and heir.

Angus and its environs had been deprived of their most powerful leader when at the start of his personal rule in 1528 James V had forfeited the Douglas earls of Angus and had begun to break up their Angus estates.[13] The re-distribution of Douglas lands benefited many of the smaller landowners in the region but overall contributed to the propagation of a complex and local society. Resultantly, family alliances and family feuds played an important part in colouring people's lives.

Left without the Douglas presence, the Lindsay earls of Crawford and the Lords Ogilvy of Airlie became the two most prominent landowners in Angus and almost the only families who had contacts, however minimal, outside the region.[14] Inter- and intra-family disputes were common and the animosity was carried over into incessant feuding between Ogilvy and Lindsay, their neighbours and part-takers.[15] This feud grew even more intense when David Lindsay of Edzell became the ninth earl of Crawford, as heir of tailze in 1542. His receipt of the title is discussed in Chapter 3 but it bears mention here because it occurred while Katherine was living at Airlie, so she must surely have been aware of the part her husband and his father took in opposing Edzell.

It is not certain when Katherine Campbell came to Airlie as a young bride. William Wilson, in his history of the Ogilvies, suggests 1536 for the marriage and sometime during 1538 for the birth of her eldest son James (later fifth Lord Ogilvy).[16] It is known that James reached the age of 18 in 1558 which suggests a marriage year of no later than 1539 for his parents. But, regardless of exactly when Katherine came to Airlie, she was not long there before the Ogilvy/Lindsay feud erupted in its greatest violence.

The earliest official recognition of Katherine Campbell's marriage to James, master of Ogilvy, is dated September 1539. In a series of grants and charters the abbot of Coupar Angus renewed the tack of the office of the bailliery of Coupar Angus to James Lord Ogilvy and his heirs male.[17] Included in this tack was a fee out of the lands of Clintlaw and Auchindorie set to James, master of Ogilvy and his spouse Katherine Campbell.[18] This entry was followed by the feu charter and precept of sasine in favour of James and Katherine to the lands above mentioned.[19] A few days later the young couple received the lands of Campsie and Craigleith from Lord Ogilvy.[20] Then in

December of that year, very possibly following the birth of a son to the master and Katherine, the original tack of the bailliery of Coupar Abbey was converted to a new hereditary lease of the office, naming the master, his wife and their children as successors to the fourth lord in the office.[21] Katherine remained the silent partner in all these transactions, but it is clear that through her marriage the Campbell influence in Angus was extending.

Katherine Campbell and James Ogilvy had five children, three boys and two girls. All five are identified together only once, when in December 1547 their mother's role as tutrix and custodian was confirmed under the privy seal.[22] Only the eldest of their sons, James, later fifth Lord Ogilvy, survived to adulthood. Of the others, Alexander, the youngest, and Archibald must have died in infancy or youth. Archibald was certainly dead before January 1563 when his mother, as executrix, brought a suit on his behalf.[23] There is no further mention of Alexander.[24] Daughters Agnes and Helen grew to adulthood with James.

Very little is known of Katherine's personal life during her marriage to the master of Ogilvie. She probably lived at Airlie Castle where she supervised the household and her growing family, but as she did so she must surely have been aware of the turbulence surrounding the lives of her men folk. Naturally, she would not have been directly involved in the feuding but she later came to know and have dealings with many of the people whose lives crossed those of her first husband's family. Not the least of these would have been David Lindsay of Edzell who later became her second husband, and his adopted son, David Lindsay, later tenth earl of Crawford, who caused her much trouble when he inherited his title.

Another likely connection from her days at Airlie may have been with Cardinal Beaton's mistress and mother of his children, Marion Ogilvy.[25] Marion was the fourth Lord Ogilvy's 'youngish' great aunt as well as the mother-in-law of David Lindsay, master and later tenth earl of Crawford.[26] Like Katherine, Marion became a single parent following the death of her children's father. She raised her family and took care of her children's affairs while living at Melgund, only a few miles away from Katherine's later home at Edzell.[27] Katherine's eldest son of her second marriage (David Lindsay of Edzell) married Marion's granddaughter, Helen Lindsay, in 1571, and in this event the two women had a common interest.[28] Marion died in 1575, just three years before Katherine and it seems highly likely that they knew one another.

As the events surrounding the Ogilvy/Lindsay feud and its resolution were unfolding, the untimely death of James V in December 1542, and the subsequent instability created by his heir's being only a few days old, threw all of Scotland into another long period of turmoil and irresolution. Factions favouring the continuation of the traditional French alliance vied with others advocating a dramatic shift to Scottish friendship with England. The split was not always entirely political either for by 1540 the Protestant Reformation had infiltrated most of Europe, including England. The political divide in Scotland became accentuated by religious preference as well. France equated with Catholic and the status quo: England with religious reform and a diplomatic shift.

When the Francophile party gained the upper hand and renounced the treaty proposing a marriage between Scotland's queen and Henry VIII's son Edward, King Henry initiated a campaign of intimidation aimed at forcing the Scots to honour the treaty.[29] These events caused the Scots to take up arms against England (or as some did, to aid and abet the English). In view of the unsettled times James master of Ogilvy took the precaution of appointing his wife Katherine as his executrix, curator and tutrix testamentary to his eldest son and their other children.[30] Katherine took the added safeguard of going to Coupar Angus abbey the next day and having her uncle Donald Campbell draw up a notarial instrument which detailed and duplicated the terms of her selection.[31] Her independent action in obtaining her own personal copy of the instrument is probably the earliest example of Katherine Campbell's acting autonomously and in her own interest. The assertive and businesslike management of her affairs, and those of her children, became characteristic of Katherine Campbell's life's work.

The years during which Katherine Campbell was living at Airlie were anything but peaceful ones either for Scotland or for her family.

A little over two years after the above arrangements were made, James master of Ogilvy was killed at the battle of Pinkie (September 1547). Katherine immediately assumed the roles and responsibilities required of her vis-à-vis her husband's estate and her children. The master's death meant that their eldest son James, then about eight or nine years old, was now heir to his grandfather. When the fourth Lord Ogilvy died two months after Pinkie, while attempting to wrest Broughty Castle from the English occupiers, James Ogilvy (Katherine's son) succeeded his grandfather, although at the time he was too young to be entered into the title.[32]

Having been given the charge to handle and make best use of her late husband's estates and monies, Katherine Campbell began to act almost immediately. With the financial assistance of Donald Campbell she purchased her son's ward and marriage from the bishop of Dunkeld in December 1547, and on the following day had her appointment as custodian/tutrix confirmed under the privy seal.[33] That she continued this active involvement in managing affairs is suggested by the fact that she borrowed money from David earl of Crawford in November 1548 and repaid him in full in less than a year. Then in December 1549 she confirmed, on behalf of her son, an annual rent of 50 merks to his uncle Thomas Ogilvy of Wester-Craig, out of the lands of Airlie. Shortly thereafter her procurator was arguing a dispute on her behalf over the superiority of the lands of Fingask (Perthshire) to which she laid claim.[34]

Concurrently, Katherine found herself at odds with her mother-in-law Helen Sinclair who, amongst other things, was refusing to deliver certain documents to Katherine as executrix and intromitter with her late husband's goods and gear.[35] Furthermore, Katherine was forced to obtain letters charging the dowager Lady Ogilvy to hand over 'the Castle, Tower, fortalice and place of Airlie' which was being withheld from her and her son James by Helen Sinclair and her younger son.[36]

James Ogilvy had three curators whose duty it was to see to his education and training for his role as fifth Lord Ogilvy.[37] The three individuals who upheld this responsibility were the boy's fraternal uncle, Thomas Ogilvy of Wester-Craig, and his maternal great uncles

Abbot Donald Campbell and John fifth Lord Erskine, Katherine's uncle by marriage.[38] Katherine might extend her interest over her son as tutrix testamentary but she lost this privilege at about the time when he reached the age of curatorship and when, at about the same time, she remarried.[39] On 21 April 1551, an assize was assembled at Airlie to value the orchards and woods of the place on behalf of James Ogilvy. The latter was represented at this event by his uncle Thomas Ogilvy, while Katherine, and her new husband, for his interest, were represented by Herbert Gledstanes.[40] Despite her re-marriage, Katherine still retained an interest in the fortunes of her eldest son. In September 1557, Donald Campbell sold to Katherine, James and his heirs the Coupar Angus lands of Meikle Forthir.[41] These became the first of several properties James was to acquire from that same source as the Reformation swept Scotland and monastic lands and offices found their way into the hands of lay people.[42]

On 10 August 1558, James Ogilvy was formally entered heir to his grandfather and in that same year he married Jean, eldest daughter of the seventh Lord Forbes and Elizabeth Keith (of Inverugie).[43] Katherine Campbell's part in the negotiations is not recorded but when she had purchased her son's ward and marriage she had received an injunction to distribute 1,500 merks of the dowry she received from James's marriage between her two Ogilvy daughters.[44] This would almost certainly ensure that she played a role in the arrangements. Furthermore, James was not yet 21 years old, and so he remained under the tutelage of his curators for another three years. (The fifth Lord Erskine had died in 1555 and it is unclear if his heir continued in the duty of curator.) James Ogilvy's paternal uncle who, according to Wilson, was not a very desirable role model[45] seems to have played an insignificant part in his nephew's life, compared with that of maternal uncle Donald Campbell, at least in the final three years of James's passage to adulthood.

It is a commonly held belief that Donald Campbell's influence brought James Ogilvy and his mother into the Protestant camp in 1559 but his father-in-law, Lord Forbes may also have played a part in shaping James's youthful behaviour.[46] The young Lord Ogilvy appeared in support of the Congregation forces at Perth and St Andrews in the summer of 1559, and throughout the following year his continued presence amongst the reformers is attested in numerous English dispatches.[47] He was present at the negotiations with the English at Berwick in the winter of 1560, when English aid was promised to the Scottish Protestants, although his title probably carried more weight than his experience in diplomacy![48] Ogilvy and Abbot Donald both attended parliament when it met in Edinburgh in August 1560 and officially changed Scotland's religion.[49] However, a year later, when the young Queen Mary landed in Scotland, James Ogilvy had reached 'perfect age' and being by then free of the constraints of his curators he chose to become a loyal queen's man.[50]

It is likely that Katherine retained some influence over her son's affairs until he came of age because of her close relationship with her uncle, James's curator. She passed on to James the lands of Meikle Forthir, purchased in his name from the abbot in 1557, while retaining a liferent to herself.[51] She defended his and her own rights to the teinds of Lintrathen in the court of the official of St Andrews in 1559 and she was forced to defend his interests in her own struggle with the tenth earl of Crawford in the early 1560s (see Chapter 4).[52] But technically and legally at least, once he had come of age, he became the head of his kin as fifth Lord Ogilvy and hereditary bailie of Coupar Angus.[53]

Meanwhile, James's two sisters Agnes and Helen Ogilvy were approaching marriageable age. Arrangements for the marriage of Agnes Ogilvy were made in October 1559 while those for Helen were concluded in January 1561.[54] The final contract for Agnes's marriage was concluded only in April 1565, at which time James Lord Ogilvy made arrangements with his mother to hand over the money for his sister's dowry referred to above.[55] Her proposed husband was the grandson of John Erskine of Dun, noted Protestant reformer and long-time associate of the earl and countess of Crawford. Dun had been the earl's man at the arbitration following the spoliation of Finavon, in 1543, and at the time of the ninth earl's death Erskine of Dun owed Crawford a substantial sum of money.[56] He continued to lean on the countess for financial assistance after she had lost her second husband, and his one extant letter to her (in her collection) gives a hint of familiarity as he complains of problems with his spendthrift son and with his sore back, the latter being the cause of his being unable to come personally to request the loan.[57]

Helen was married to John Ogilvy of Inverquharity, sometimes called the young laird of Inverquharity. There were undoubtedly connections of kinship in this arrangement, and certainly Katherine Campbell had confidence in the young laird's father. He was her representative when she agreed to arbitration in one dispute and they had other business in common for they entered into an obligation together in November 1560 that was discharged four months later.[58] Furthermore, she had a gold chain belonging to him in her possession taken in pledge for money he had borrowed from her.[59] In this case, as with Agnes's marriage, the parties were all familiar with one another and were 'old family friends'.

These three marriages stood the test of time. Katherine respected James, now fifth Lord Ogilvy's position as head of the family. There was frequent and necessary communication between the two in inheritance matters and in many financial transactions.[60] But overall, Katherine seems not to have had a particularly close relationship with James, his wife and their nine children. Katherine remained dutiful and businesslike with her eldest son, but as her testamentary papers reveal, she did not trust him.[61] In contrast, there appears to have been a warm relationship between mother, daughters and their spouses. The details concerning the later relationships between Katherine and all of her children will be discussed more fully in Chapter 5.

Katherine Campbell passed almost three years as the dowager mistress of Ogilvy. Sometime during the summer months of 1550 she was married for a second time and moved from Airlie to Edzell, the home of her new husband David Lindsay of Edzell, ninth earl of Crawford. Her Ogilvy children were still under age in 1550 and much of what has been recounted here about them took place during or following her second marriage.

NOTES

1. E. Cowan, 'The Angus Campbells and the origins of the Campbell-Ogilvie Feud', in *Scottish Studies*, 25 (1981), 28.

2. J. Dawson, *The Politics of Religion in the Reign of Mary, Queen of Scots* (Cambridge, 2002), 19, 81.

3. *The Letters of King James V,* ed. R.K. Hannay, (SHS, 1954), 199; *Rentale of the Cistercian Abbey of Cupar-Angus,* ed. C. Rogers (Grampian Club, 1879), hereafter cited as *Rentale,* intro. p. 1 (50) where the editor notes Cardinal Wolsey's assistance in influencing the appointment.

4. F. Bardgett, *Scotland Reformed: The Reformation in Angus and the Mearns* (Edinburgh, 1989), 54, n.70.

5. M. Sanderson, *Scottish Rural Society in the Sixteenth Century* (Edinburgh, 1982), 93; Cowan, 'Angus Campbells', 31. The house of Hamilton also found positions in the church to be profitable and used these as platforms for extending family influence: E. Finnie, 'The House of Hamilton: Patronage, Politics and the Church in the Reformation Period', *IR,* 36 (1985), 10-14.

6. Cowan, 'Angus Campbells', 28.

7. Dawson, *Politics of Religion,* 81; Reddington-Wilde, 'A Woman's Place', 206.

8. The Douglas Earls of Angus had been forfeited by King James when he took personal control in 1528, leaving a vacuum in power in Angus which was filled by the Lindsay earls of Crawford and the Lords Ogilvy of Airlie.

9. Dawson, *Politics of Religion,* 62.

10. Bardgett, *Scotland Reformed,* 3.

11. *Scots Peerage,* i (Ogilvy of Airlie) and vii (Sinclair, Lord Sinclair).

12. *Ibid.,* iii, 27; 'Papers from the Charter Chest at Dun' in *The Miscellany of the Spalding Club,* ed. John Stuart (Spalding Club, 1849), iv, p. lxxvii notes a reference to her death in 1538.

13. J. Cameron, *James V: The personal Rule 1528-1542* (East Linton, 1998), esp. ch. 3.

14. Bardgett, *Scotland Reformed,* 12. These in no way matched the kin/affinity groups to which the great earls like Argyll or Huntly could lay claim.

15. NAS, Airlie Muniments, GD16/41/8,9,12; NLS, The Haigh Inventory, Box E II nos. 7-10.

16. W. Wilson, *The House of Airlie,* 3 vols. (London, 1924), i, 103, 108.

17. NAS, Airlie Muniments, GD16/25/74, and printed in *Charters of the Abbey of Coupar Angus,* ed., D. Easson, 2 vols. (SHS, 1947), ii, 151-5.

18. *Ibid.*

19. *Ibid.,* 156-61. Note the presence of Katherine's father as a witness to this charter.

20. Wilson, *House,* i, 103.

21 NAS, Airlie Muniments, GD16/25/75.

22 *RSS*, iii, 411-12 no. 2572.

23 NLS, The Haigh Inventory, Box E II no. 97.

24 Scots Peerage i, 118. Their names, Archibald and Alexander, are the same as the names ascribed to sons of the fourth Lord Ogilvy in this source.

25 M. Sanderson, *Mary Stewart's People: Life in Mary Stewart's* Scotland (Edinburgh, 1987), ch. 1. The Ogilvies were hereditary bailies of Beaton's abbey at Arbroath.

26 *Ibid.*, 4.

27 Marion was at Edzell in 1556 as a member of a panel arbitrating a dispute involving one of her daughters: *Ibid.*, 15.

28 NLS, Crawford Muniments, 4/1/80-84.

29 For a full discussion of the complexities of this period 1542-47, see M. Merriman, *The Rough Wooings: Mary Queen of Scots 1542-1551* (East Linton, 2000).

30 NAS, Airlie Muniments, GD16/24/178 (July 1545). It was quite common for wives to be so designated: Sanderson, *A Kindly Place?*, 114; Finlay, 'Women and Legal Representation', 167.

31 NAS, Airlie Muniments, GD16/43/1.

32 Meanwhile, Katherine's clan chief the earl of Argyll was negotiating with the English to call off the siege of Broughty in exchange for a bribe: *CSPS*, i, 71-72 no. 148 (Feb. 1548). Donald Campbell and Katherine's father were also caught up in the business at Broughty. Donald raised a troop of 150 at one point and at another offered the monastery at Coupar Angus as the location for a meeting between Argyll and the English: *ibid.*, 87 no. 176, 93-96 no. 192.

33 NAS, Airlie Muniments, GD16/42/12, 1 and 2; *RSS*, iii, 411-12 no. 2572.

34 NAS, Airlie Muniments, GD16/42/14, borrowing from the earl of Crawford; *RMS*, iv, 128 no. 567, grant to Thomas Ogilvy dated 17 Dec. 1549, confirmed 8 Feb. 1551; NAS, Perth Sheriff Court Records, SC49/1/1, fo. 122v. Mr Alexander McBrek, who was her procurator, was a burgess of Perth, tenant in Campsie and a close associate of the abbot of Coupar Angus.

35 NLS, The Haigh Inventory, Box E II nos. 21, 23, 25, 27 (this last document dated June 1550!).

36 *Ibid.*, no. 22. Harris noted that it was common amongst widowed English noblewomen to have difficulty securing the property and goods due to them: *English Aristocratic Women*, 134-5.

37 NAS, Airlie Muniments, GD16/24/178.

38 Erskine's wife was a daughter of the second earl of Argyll and sister to Donald Campbell and to Katherine's father: *Scots Peerage*, v, 610.

39 Coutts, 'Wife and Widow', 177-8.

40 NAS, Airlie Muniments, GD16/41/16. Gledstanes was a longtime and trusted servant of Katherine and the earl of Crawford.

41   *Ibid.*, GD16/28/11a and 11b. These lands had been tacked to Katherine and the master of Ogilvy in 1546: NLS, The Haigh Inventory Box E II no. 19.

42   See also Wilson, *House,* i, 115-16; *Charters of Coupar Angus,* ii, 230, 232; *Rentale,* ii, 175.

43   NAS, Airlie Muniments, GD16/41/20. Forbes and Keith associations lay to the north in Aberdeenshire rather than in Angus, although Katherine's sister was married to Forbes of Towie.

44   *RSS,* iii, 411-12 no. 2572 (1,000 merks was to go to the elder daughter Agnes and 500 merks to Helen, the younger of the two).

45   Wilson, *House,* i, 104-5.

46   Bardgett, *Scotland Reformed,* 73. The Scottish Reformation rebellion began overtly in May 1559. Forbes was reported to be uncommitted according to English dispatches (*CSPS,* i, 220 no. 480) although Wilson claims that the Forbeses were a strong Protestant family: *House,* i, 149.

47   *CSPS,* i, 218 no. 474, 220 no. 480, 383 no. 751, 385 no. 754, 403 no. 786.

48   Wilson, *House,* i, 113, but Ogilvy is not mentioned in the English dispatch, *CSPS,* i, 324 no. 665

49   *Ibid.,* 458 no. 879.

50   Wilson, *House,* i, 115. (Not to mention to end his days as a Catholic.) G. Donaldson, *All The Queen's Men: Power Politics in Mary Stewart's Scotland* (London, 1983), passim.

51   NLS, The Haigh Inventory, Box E II no. 19 (1546); NAS, Airlie Muniments, GD16/28/11 (Sept. 1559).

52   *Ibid.,* GD 16/41/21.

53   NLS, The Haigh Inventory, Box E II no. 97. In 1563, his mother required him to convene a court as Bailie of Coupar Angus in her pursuit of one of her interests.

54   *Ibid.,* Box E II no. 65 accompanied by a note in the margin of the inventory that the document is now missing. Both marriages are referred to in relation to oversight of the girls' dowries: *The Clan Campbell,* ed. H. Paton, 8 vols. (Edinburgh, 1913-1922), vi, 42 where the author notes that Helen's contract was not registered until May 1583.

55   NAS, Erskine of Dun Muniments, GD123/140 where there are three copies of the contract dated 13 April 1565; NLS, The Haigh Inventory, Box E II no. 123 is James Lord Ogilvy's April 1565 commitment to hand over the dowry money to his mother.

56   See Chapter 2; NLS, Crawford Muniments, 1/1/14.

57   *Ibid.,* 3/1/4.

58   NLS, The Haigh Inventory, Box E II no 184; NAS, Register of Deeds, RD1/4, fos. 2r-2v, 76r-76v.

59   NLS, Crawford Muniments, 3/1/16.

60   NLS, The Haigh Inventory, Box E II no. 124, Katherine took a tack (lease) of

some lands from James; NAS, Airlie Muniments, GD16/29/20, discharge by Katherine to James of part of a debt he owed to her.

[61] The evidence for this assessment is discussed in Chapter 5. It can be read into NLS, Crawford Muniments, 3/1/14-22.

Table 1.1

Ogilvy Sons and Daughters

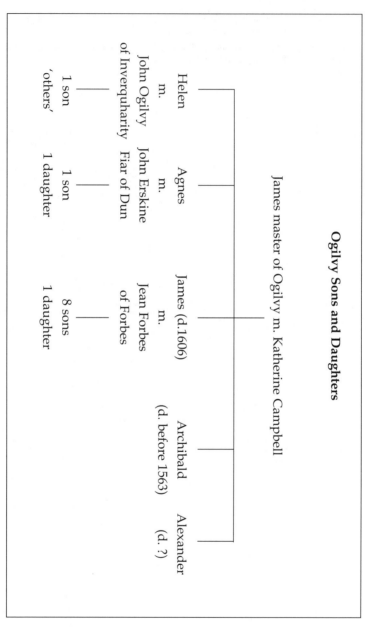

James master of Ogilvy m. Katherine Campbell

Helen
m.
John Ogilvy
of Inverquharity

Agnes
m.
John Erskine
Fiar of Dun

James (d.1606)
m.
Jean Forbes
of Forbes

Archibald
(d. before 1563)

Alexander
(d. ?)

1 son
'others'

1 son
1 daughter

8 sons
1 daughter

2

KATHERINE CAMPBELL, COUNTESS OF CRAWFORD

When Katherine Campbell became countess of Crawford her new husband the ninth earl had recently lost his first wife and had no children of his own. He had an antagonistic adopted son who would succeed to the title upon his death, and he faced numerous other problems caused by his own rather precarious position. He had inherited the earldom as nearest heir following the forfeiture of the eighth earl's son and grandson, and he had to contend with legal and financial difficulties as well as with his troublesome heir. To shed some light on this web of controversy and animosity into which Katherine married and with which she had to deal long after the ninth earl had passed away it seems necessary to provide a brief introduction to the fortunes of the earldom of Crawford during the first half of the sixteenth century. Many of the issues with which Katherine was forced to deal throughout the 1560s and 70s grew out of events that had taken place before she came to Edzell.

The Lindsay Earls of Crawford

The earldom of Crawford had been experiencing severe financial difficulties since the late fifteenth century when the sixth earl of Crawford was unable to claim his title of duke of Montrose and was forced to dispose of the sheriffship of Aberdeen as well.[1] The sixth earl was killed at Flodden and his heir followed him to the grave a mere four years later, passing the title to David, eighth earl of Crawford in 1517.

During the personal rule of James V, i.e. from 1528 onwards, the earldom of Crawford, along with several other estates and their holders in the region, became subject to royal interference and pressure as the king attempted to 'destabilise the earls of Angus' influence there'.[2] Taking advantage of Crawford's financial weakness, and of his alleged support of Angus, a judgment was brought by the Lords of Council in May 1532 that found that the seventh earl of Crawford had been improperly served after Flodden and consequently that the eighth earl's infeftment was likewise invalid. This decision by the lords resulted in the pursuit of the eighth earl for non-entry and associated fees, dating back to 1513, leaving the estate vulnerable and at the disposal of the crown.[3] Although the eighth earl managed to reach an agreement with the crown to purchase the non-entry, his commitment placed a serious financial burden on the estate. He sold some of his already mortgaged lands, and mortgaged much of the rest of the estate. He even required some of his principal tenants to pay their portions of the non-entry, resulting in what Jamie Cameron referred to as the 'legal emasculation' of the earldom.[4]

In addition to his predicament with the crown, the eighth earl was burdened with a troublesome son and heir, Alexander Lindsay, dubbed 'the wicked master'. Having been put in fee of the earldom by his father in 1527, the young heir embarked on a career of oppressing and alienating the lands of the earldom. He attacked and imprisoned his father and others of his kin, most notably for our purposes, David Lindsay of Edzell.[5] Alexander was censured, reprieved, and then continuing his evil behaviour, he was required to renounce his rights to the earldom of Crawford in March 1537. Although his life was spared the forfeiture took effect, excluding him and his heirs from any right or claim to the title.[6]

According to Scottish law, title to the earldom reverted to the next male heir in the succession, the eighth earl's second cousin once-removed David Lindsay of Edzell.[7] Three weeks prior to his receiving a charter of the earldom, Edzell entered into an obligation with King James to take possession on condition that his heirs resign it into the king's hands when and if required to do so by the king, under penalty of a huge fine for default.[8] Historians and others differ on their interpretations of this gesture, ranging from the manipulations of a covetous and acquisitive monarch to expert legal practice executed on behalf of the crown. Jamie Cameron concluded that Edzell's obligation to the king 'was intended to leave open the option of succession for Alexander's heirs'.[9] Certainly in 1541, Alexander had a son and heir in the person of David Lindsay, as well as two daughters, born to him and his wife Jean Sinclair, while Lindsay of Edzell had no children. The eighth earl had enjoyed the support of Edzell over the years and when Alexander, the 'wicked master', was killed in a brawl in Dundee (sometime after July 1541) the way seemed clear for the ageing earl to entail the earldom in favour of Edzell.[10] Thus, when the eighth earl died in November 1542, David Lindsay of Edzell duly paid 4,000 merks to the crown to be served heir.[11]

Upon the death of King James in December 1542, Edzell had quickly and quietly withdrawn his bond of resignation 'ad perpetuam remanentiam' in January 1543. For a while it remained unnoticed but somehow the new governor, the earl of Arran, got wind of the original obligation and required the treasurer to surrender a copy to him. It is possible that Arran sought to enforce its terms but he accepted an acquittance of 7,000 merks as the price of a discharge.[12] David Lindsay of Edzell then moved forward to deal with the opposition to his infeftment. There were some lords and men in Angus and its environs who refused to acknowledge Lindsay of Edzell as the rightful heir to the earldom of Crawford. They preferred instead to uphold the rights of the direct, and in their eyes legitimate heir, David Lindsay, grandson of the eighth earl. James Lord Ogilvy of Airlie and his son, their kin and friends, were chief amongst the younger David's partisans.[13] They captured the young man and in his name began a campaign of harassment against the new earl.

The spoliation of Finavon, home of the earls of Crawford, was begun in October 1542, shortly before the eighth earl died. Judging from the summons considerable numbers of livestock, crops, wood and fruit-bearing trees were destroyed.[14] The contents of the house with its furniture and furnishings were ruined, including beds, doors, locks and sixteen great glass windows. The chapel lost vestments of fine silk, velvet and damask as well as a silver chalice and other ornaments. Money, wine and weapons were uplifted resulting in a total ransacking of the house. A summons, raised by the earl against the perpetrators, only caused further violence directed against Edzell's own family house at Glenesk which underwent similar treatment. Royal letters purchased by the earl eventually charged Lord Ogilvy and his accomplices to cease and desist.[15] Arbitration between the parties was eventually arranged in 1543, John Erskine of Dun representing the earl of Crawford and James Lord Ogilvy representing the dispossessed David Lindsay. This resulted in each side discharging the other and the master of Ogilvy agreeing to restore Finavon.[16] The instrument on the discharge by the earl of Crawford makes it eminently clear that the master of Ogilvy was the ringleader in the spoliation of the home of the earls of Crawford.[17]

It is generally agreed that this arbitration resulted in a series of contracts, bonds and obligations negotiated between all of the factions that culminated in the marriage of the young David Lindsay in 1546. By that time Cardinal David Beaton had intruded himself into the affair. Beaton's interference could be taken as a sign of his concern for his allies who were also the hereditary bailies (chief executive officers) of his abbey at Arbroath, but it appears more likely that he saw some advantage to 'extending his position in his own locale' by becoming involved.[18] For David Lindsay of Edzell, his obligation of September 1541, though officially withdrawn, may have played into the arrangements worked out by 1546, for he himself remained childless and without an heir.

On 10 April 1546 a contract of marriage was negotiated between David Lindsay, grandson of the eighth earl of Crawford, and Margaret Beaton, daughter of Cardinal David Beaton and Marion Ogilvy. By the terms of the contract Margaret's tocher of 4,000 merks (£2,666 13s 4d) was to be paid by the cardinal to the earl of Crawford.[19] The marriage was duly solemnized within the month and the ninth earl of Crawford adopted David Lindsay, the eighth earl's grandson, reinstating him as master of and heir to the earldom of Crawford.[20] The ninth earl thus became liferenter of the title, which might only revert to his own Edzell branch of the family on the failure of the young master's heirs. Furthermore, by the terms of the agreement, the ninth earl retained the superiority of his own lands of Glenesk, Fern, Dalbog and Newdosk which were to remain within the house of Edzell and were not to be consolidated with the earldom's lands until the master came of age. In exchange for his adoption and reinstatement, the new master gave his bond to the earl, whereby he agreed to the entail of the estate should he (the former) die without heirs.[21]

Despite the lengthy contracts, bonds and assurances, the new master of Crawford did little to endear himself to his benefactor. Within three years of the marriage negotiations and adoption agreements David, master of Crawford was provoking the ninth earl, his neighbours and tenants.[22] The earl pursued civil and canonical legal actions against the master obtaining letters of horning and cursing against him for breach of contract, but the master retaliated by causing the cursing of the earl.[23] Manoeuvres such as these continued throughout 1550 and 1551 by which time, the earl's circumstances had been considerably altered by his marriage to Katherine Campbell who delivered to him a son and heir in the person of yet another David Lindsay!

Consequently when the young master of Crawford came of age, the ninth earl was unwilling to live up to his agreement to resign the superiority of Edzell to him.[24] The agreement of 1546 was not registered as promised, causing the master to begin a new round of actions against the earl to force the return of the superiority of Edzell to Crawford. The master claimed that he had been cheated out of his rightful revenues since the agreement had not been registered. The earl, for his part, now had a son and heir and although there is no evidence to suggest that he made any claim to the earldom of Crawford for this boy, he certainly wanted his own patrimonial lands to pass to his own son.[25] That the earl neglected to register this agreement was surely motivated by personal interest, for by 1551 he had good reason to keep separate the lands of Edzell for his son and heir.[26]

In the end and after almost seven years of argument the earl was judged to have failed to register the agreement and was ordered into ward in 1557. At this juncture the queen regent, Mary of Guise, intervened in his demise and ordered that the original judgment of ward in Dumbarton be mitigated to ward in Edinburgh Castle because, she claimed, Dumbarton Castle was too cold and damp.[27] Either imprisonment, concern for his health or the prospect of death caused the ninth earl of Crawford to come to an agreement with his adopted son on 16 March 1558. The contemporary evidence for this bargain is lacking although negotiations were definitely underway throughout 1557.[28] Furthermore, in the lengthy obligation drawn by David Lindsay (of Glenesk) prior to his marriage to the tenth earl's daughter in March 1571, the details regarding the exception of the lands of Edzell are spelled out and specific reference is made to the agreement between the ninth earl and the master in March 1558.[29] Perhaps after the agreement had been reached the earl was discharged from his confinement but he had not long to live. He gave up his testament at his castle of Invermark on 20 September 1558, and died before the end of that month.[30] A debt owed by the earl and registered in his testament suggests that at the time of his death David Lindsay of Edzell was indeed buying out the lands of Edzell for he owed 'David, once master now Crawford' £1,733 6s 8d 'for the redemption of lands'.[31]

The Countess of Crawford

In mid-September 1547, Katherine Campbell found herself a widow after about nine or ten years of marriage to the master of Ogilvy. Three years later she became countess of Crawford as the wife of David Lindsay of Edzell, ninth earl of Crawford. Lords, lairds and noblemen in sixteenth-century Scotland regarded marriage as a means to serve the family and to promote its interests. Although personal feelings and preferences might be taken into account, the final decision was based on the interests of the families involved rather than on the individuals.[32]

The fourth earl of Argyll was the most senior member of Katherine Campbell's kin group in 1547 and as such it was he, most likely, who approved the arrangements for her second marriage to the earl of Crawford.[33] There were probably good reasons to have Katherine remain in Angus, for she was the mother of the heir to

Airlie, and her terce lands were mainly located in the region. It was also evident by 1548 that she and her uncle Donald Campbell, abbot of Coupar Angus, worked well together. Consequently another marriage within the same region would keep them in close proximity and would continue to serve the Campbell interests favourably. Conveniently, the ninth earl of Crawford had just lost his first wife in February 1550.[34] His availability, not to mention his influential position, made him an attractive choice for a marriage with Argyll's second cousin.

Katherine married David Lindsay of Edzell, ninth earl of Crawford, and became countess of Crawford after 10 June and before 12 November 1550. The earl's first wife Jonet Gray died in February 1550. Katherine's brother John, commendator of Ardchattan, referred to her as his dearest sister and 'mistress of Ogilvy', when he gave her a three year tack of the teinds of Kilbrandane, on 10 June of that year.[35] On 12 November a charter infefting Katherine in a conjoint fee of the barony of Ferne and other lands in Forfar was confirmed under the great seal.[36] Katherine had become countess of Crawford.

David Lindsay of Edzell, ninth earl of Crawford, and Katherine Campbell probably knew one another for some time before their marriage. While at Airlie, she may well have attended the festivities reputed to have been celebrated with 'considerable pomp and magnificence' in honour of the marriage of Margaret Beaton to David Lindsay.[37] She would most likely have met the ninth earl of Crawford at that gathering, if she had not already done so before that date. Certainly after her husband was killed at Pinkie she had business dealings with the earl as on the occasion when she borrowed £200 from him in 1548 and repaid him for the loan the following year.[38]

Katherine Campbell and David Lindsay's marriage seems to have been mutually congenial and in its brief course, Katherine gave birth to seven children, five boys and two girls. These children must have arrived in quick succession for the marriage ended with the earl's death only eight years after it had been entered into.[39] It could be assumed that possibly the youngest, Margaret, was born posthumously, and Katherine confirmed this some months after her husband's death when she apologised to the sheriff of Forfar for her inability to appear in his court as charged because 'we ar bot laitlie delyvereit of ane barne'.[40]

Katherine was, for the most part, a witness to rather then a direct participant in her husband's clash with his adopted son, but she must have been emotionally involved when David was imprisoned in 1557. In other business matters, however, during the years of her marriage to the earl of Crawford, Katherine Campbell played a very visible role. As his spouse she was regularly named in grants and charters to recovered and newly-acquired lands, as well as in contracts, loans and other business entered into by the earl.[41] By means of all her involvement, she undoubtedly acquired the skills and habits which were both practical and necessary to her when she had to manage property and people on her own.

Quite naturally she was directly involved in affairs that would affect her (and David Lindsay's) children in the matter of their inheritances. Both the earl and the countess made conscious efforts to provide for their children. This was common wisdom for people in their position for in early modern Scotland land provided a noble house with its identity. Land equalled wealth and superiority over territory, attributes that were far more important than how the land was used.[42] It therefore behoved the earl to acquire land and incomes for his house and for his children. This he did consistently, in conjunction with his wife, throughout the 1550s and after his death Katherine kept up the practice of acquiring property and other forms of income that could be passed on to their younger sons.[43]

David Lindsay of Glenesk, afterwards Sir David Lindsay of Edzell, was the eldest of Katherine's Lindsay children. His brothers were John, Walter, James, and Robert and his sisters were Elizabeth and Margaret. All survived to adulthood and all remained under the tutelage of their mother following the death of their father in 1558, for she had been appointed sole executrix and tutrix to those alive or to be born to the couple in February 1555.[44] Katherine's relationships with these children as maturing adults are the subject of a later section of this work.

The first-born, David Lindsay, was entered heir presumptive to all the lands of Edzell on 1 April 1554 with the appropriate reservations for the upkeep of his parents.[45] Because the ninth earl had committed himself to returning the earldom to the direct line in 1546, his eldest son by Katherine Campbell simply became heir to Edzell, to the lordship of Glenesk and to the lands of Fern, Dalbog and Newdosk. He had no claim to the earldom of Crawford and in fact made no attempt to make such a claim. Katherine must have known that should she and the earl have a son that he would not inherit his father's title of earl, but one still wonders whether or not she was disappointed for him, especially when the master so persistently provoked his benefactor and her husband the ninth earl.

The earl's conflict with the master can be explained in part by his desire to pass on his own lands and title to his own son, despite his earlier commitment to the adopted one. His refusal to register the contract with the master and his intransigence throughout the prolonged debate, at considerable personal risk, meant that his eldest son's future was ensured. David Lindsay would become laird of Edzell. That being settled, there were several other sons whose survival necessitated their parents' securing livelihoods for each one.

To meet this challenge the earl and his wife began to acquire incomes from various sources. They purchased lands outright from those willing to or needful of selling their property. These properties were not part of the entailed lands and were added to when the earl and countess procured escheats, non-entrances and the ward and marriage of minors. Many of these acquisitions were taken up by the parents in liferent to themselves and in heritable tenure to sons David, John or Walter. Much of what eventually became the patrimony of the younger sons James and Robert was acquired by their mother in the 1560s. Her pattern of acquisition remained the same and no doubt she had learned valuable lessons as she worked alongside her second husband to ensure the futures of their sons.

All of these purchases are too numerous to detail here, but just to illustrate with a few examples: in 1553, the earl acquired land in July, October, November and December.[46] Additionally, the couple took advantage of the inability of David Lindsay of the Haugh of Finavon to purchase his entry to his lands by drawing up a contract with him in April of that year which eventually, after many years of argument, resulted in son Walter's becoming the possessor of the lands and the accompanying office of hereditary keeper of the castle of Finavon.[47] The year 1555 was another one in which numerous purchases were made including the lands of Balhalwell, Auchneves and Makindob.[48] In the spring they exchanged some property in Aberdeenshire for lands closer to home in the barony of Ferne.[49] They then purchased the rights to the parsonage of Finavon, served by a rector named Mr David Lindsay to whom the earl owed money at the time of his death.[50] The rector subsequently tacked the teinds of the parsonage to them.[51] The earl and countess also purchased the teinds of several other parishes including Newdosk, Lethnot and Lochlee,[52] and they entered into an arrangement with the dean and chapter of Brechin Cathedral which brought them various lands and incomes in heritable feu.[53] They were perhaps fortunate to be in need of lands and incomes at that particular time when ecclesiastical lands were so readily available. Once having acquired all of the above, they had frequently to face the disapproval of tenants who manifested their animosity by withholding rents or destroying the crops. These actions by the tenants caused the earl and countess to initiate suits in court to collect delinquent rents in kind and money.[54]

The year 1558 was a most eventful and certainly a highly emotional one in the life of Katherine Campbell. Her husband, having agreed to terms with the master of Crawford, was released from ward. A few months later, on 20 September 1558, he was at Invermark where he appointed his wife his executrix, intromissioner with all his goods and custodian of their children. He then dictated his testament, commending his soul to God and requesting burial in 'his' aisle in the church at Edzell.[55] He died at Michaelmas and ten days later Katherine gave up his testament at Edzell. Sometime thereafter (the date is illegible) she sought a discharge for having carried out her duties as executrix.[56]

Just two months after the loss of her husband, death claimed the life of the fourth earl of Argyll, Katherine's cousin and chief of her clan. This loss may have been less intensely personal for Katherine, but widowed as she was by then, her senior male kinsman became a key player in shaping her future. Archibald, fifth earl of Argyll was considerably younger than Katherine and he quickly became an influential participant in national politics as well as in determining the affairs of his kin and family.[57] In that same year, James Ogilvy of Airlie was entered heir to his grandfather as fifth Lord Ogilvy and was married to Jean Forbes. He would have been about 18 years old at the time and he remained under the tutelage of his curators for another three years, although in becoming head of his family he took precedence over his mother in matters concerning his sisters.

Thus, at then end of 1558, Katherine Campbell found herself a widow once again, with seven under-aged children, two teenaged daughters almost eligible for marriages and a clan chief considerably her junior who held her uncertain future in his gift. And these were not the only uncertainties facing her. The year 1558 had also produced some significant political shifts for all the people of Scotland. Their young Queen Mary had married Francis, Dauphin of France and while her mother, Mary of Guise, strove to hold on to her daughter's Scottish heritage, the threat of prolonged French (and by implication Catholic) influence caused grave concern amongst certain Scottish noblemen. Some indeed had gone so far as to adopt a bond (December 1557) to support one another in furthering the cause of Protestantism in Scotland.[58] One of the signatories to this bond was Katherine's cousin the fourth earl of Argyll who on his deathbed elicited from his son and heir a solemn promise to press ahead with the demand for religious reform in Scotland.[59] Consequently the fifth earl of Argyll became a leader amongst Scottish Protestants: an affiliation and cause that would impact on his kin who were his agents in Angus, Donald, abbot of Coupar Angus and Katherine, now dowager countess of Crawford.

As she had done for James Ogilvy, Katherine purchased David Lindsay's ward and marriage,[60] and thereafter continued the work she and her late husband had already begun of acquiring lands and incomes for her children. One curious document in the collection of Katherine Campbell's personal papers from this period (October 1559) is a precept for absolution for 'ecclesiastical causes' granted to Lady Katherine Campbell and delivered to her from the deacon of Brechin.[61] This brief five and a half line document does not specify what were the 'causes' but it seems possible that the now tenth earl's pursuit of the ninth earl in the ecclesiastical courts had resulted in the excommunication of both husband and wife. Since their joint partnership in affairs was commonplace throughout the 1550s a ban of excommunication may have been raised on both, requiring Katherine's release therefrom in 1559.

The most immediate problems facing the dowager countess in the early 1560s were serious ones involving her extended family. The new earl of Crawford was by far the most belligerent person Katherine had to deal with, but she was also confronted by some of her Campbell kin, most notably the earl of Argyll who was always civil, but insistent and by the heirs of her uncle Donald, abbot of Coupar Angus, one of whom was particularly difficult. In addition, Katherine Campbell had her late husband's testament to administer, her children's lands to manage and defend, their educations to attend to and their marriages to arrange. There was no time to be wasted and none to grieve as she quickly found out. The dowager countess proved to be more than capable of taking on these challenges as the next chapters reveal.

NOTES

[1] Lord Lindsay, *Lives of the Lindsays*, 3 vols. (London, 1858), i, 180-1; Bardgett, *Scotland Reformed*, 10.

[2] Cameron, *James V*, 113.

[3] *Ibid.*, 109; for a full analysis of 'The Crawford Case' see *ibid.*, 106-13, 278-79.

[4] *Ibid.*, 110.

[5] *Ibid.*, 107; Bardgett, *Scotland Reformed*, 10-11.

[6] Lindsay, *Lives*, i, 194-7; NLS, The Haigh Inventory, Box B no. 251.

[7] Cameron, *James V*, 278.

[8] NLS, The Haigh Inventory, Box E no. 293 (28 September 1544).

[9] Cameron, *James V*, 279.

[10] *RMS*, iii, 569-70 no. 2484; NLS, Crawford Muniments, 1/1/7.

[11] Cameron, *James V*, 278.

[12] *Ibid.*, 279; Lindsay, *Lives*, i, 199.

[13] And, it should be recalled, the fourth Lord Ogilvy's wife and the mother of the dispossessed heir were sisters.

[14] NLS, The Haigh Inventory, Box B no. 262, Box E nos. 144, 147.

[15] *Ibid.*, Box B no. 301, Box C nos. 1, 2.

[16] NAS, Airlie Muniments, GD16/41/14; NLS, The Haigh Inventory, Box E no. 300; Lindsay, *Lives*, i, 198.

[17] *Miscellany of the Spalding Club*, iv, 119-120.

[18] M. Sanderson, *Cardinal of Scotland David Beaton c.1494-1546* (Edinburgh 1986), 221.

[19] *Ibid.*, 221-2; NLS, The Haigh Inventory, Box C nos. 3-5.

[20] *Ibid.*, Box E no. 262 (registered 16 March 1547); Lindsay, *Lives*, i, 198.

[21] 2 May 1546, *RMS*, iii, 756 no. 3231; Cameron, *James V*, 279 concluded that the whole affair was an 'opportunity for financial exploitation by the crown'.

[22] NLS, The Haigh Inventory, Box C nos. 20-29, Box E no. 240.

[23] *Ibid.*, nos. 174, 336-38.

[24] *Ibid.*, no. 342.

[25] *Ibid.*, no. 343 is a document entitled, 'Information for the Earl of Crawford for stopping of the registering the pretended contract made at Edzell betwixt him and David Master of Crawford, of date 14 April 1551'.

[26] NLS, The Haigh Inventory, Box E 332-369, (litigation 1543-57); Bardgett, *Scotland Reformed*, 54-55. Although it does not justify the ninth earl's failure to live up to his obligation, he had worked judiciously throughout his term as earl to redeem the lands of the earldom, sold and wadset by his predecessor: NLS, The Haigh Inventory, Box A nos. 11, 12, 13, 16, 17.

[27] NLS, Crawford Muniments, 1/1/13.

[28] NLS, The Haigh Inventory, Box E nos. 350-368.

[29] NLS, Crawford Muniments, 4/1/80; NAS, Register of Deeds, RD1/11, fos. 358v –362r with specific reference at fo. 359v.

[30] NLS, Crawford Muniments, 1/1/14.

[31] *Ibid.*

[32] *Campbell Letters*, 28-34; Sanderson, *A Kindly Place?*, esp. ch. 8 for the experience of sixteenth-century Scottish women; Harris, *English Aristocratic Women*, 55, 70.

[33] *Campbell Letters*, 28; Dawson, *Politics of Religion*, 81.

[34] NLS, Crawford Muniments, 2/1/1; The Haigh Inventory, Box E II no. 14.

[35] *Ibid.,* no. 26.

[36] *RMS,* iv, 122 no. 539; NLS, The Haigh Inventory, Box E nos. 121, 122. Others followed in March 1552: *ibid.,* nos. 241-245.

[37] Sanderson, *Mary Stewart's People,* 12.

[38] NAS, Airlie Miniments, GD16/42/14.

[39] Frequent pregnancies amongst Scottish elite women were typical and were a result of the mother's not breastfeeding her own infant but rather making use of a wet nurse. M. Meikle in her forthcoming provisionally titled *Scotland in the long 16th Century.* (Edinburgh, 2007) Chapter 2, addresses 'Women and children in Scottish Society', part iv, 'Childbirth'.

[40] NLS, The Haigh Inventory, Box E II no. 53 (12 March, 1559).

[41] NAS, RD1/2, fos. 318v-321v, fos. 359v-360r, 399r.

[42] Dawson, *Politics of Religion,* 68-69.

[43] NLS, The Haigh Inventory, Box E nos. 138, 166, 249, 250 as just some examples from the year 1555. Harris, *English Aristocratic Women*, 64-7, 144, 160, found English noblewomen acquired business and legal skills by working alongside their spouses.

[44] NLS, The Haigh Inventory, Box E II no. 34.

[45] *RMS,* iv, 206, no. 922; NLS, The Haigh Inventory, Box F no. 23. Another son, Walter, was alive in October 1553 when he was identified as a beneficiary of a grant: *RSS,* iv, 362-3 no. 2187, (30 October 1553). Walter was in fact the third son of the union.

[46] NLS, The Haigh Inventory, Box E no. 125, Box E II nos. 30, 265; NAS, Acts and Decreets of the Lords of Council and Session (herafter ADCS), CS7/8, fos. 406r-408r.

[47] NLS, The Haigh Inventory, Box E no. 247, Box E II no. 36. The affair of the Haugh went on for many years and as a widow Katherine had to continue pursuit of David Lindsay for acknowledgement of his agreements with the earl and countess which followed upon this original contract.

[48] *Ibid.,* Box E nos. 110, 275, 249, 250. The Balhallwell agreement was subsequently

recorded in the Register of Deeds, NAS, RD1/1, fo. 124v.

[49] *RMS,* iv, 222 no. 223.

[50] NLS, The Haigh Inventory, Box E no. 138; Crawford Muniments, 1/1/14.

[51] Bardgett, *Scotland Reformed,* 57 n 95-7.

[52] NLS, The Haigh Inventory, Box, E no. 166, (Newdosk), Box F no. 164, (Lethnot and Lochlee).

[53] *RMS,* v, 283-5 no. 884 (Confirmation, on 20 August 1585, of five charters dating from 1554-1557, to David Lindsay of Edzell).

[54] NLS, The Haigh Inventory, Box E nos. 273-86 for some examples.

[55] NLS, Crawford Muniments, 1/1/14. His first wife was laid to rest in the parish church of Edzell as well: *ibid.,* 2 /1/1.

[56] *Ibid.,* 1/1/18. She may have requested the discharge at this time or this document may have been drawn up by her in 1575 when her children and others questioned her intromissions with her late husband's assets and debts: NLS, The Haigh Inventory, Box E II nos. 205, 210, 216.

[57] *Campbell Letters,* 165.

[58] *Ibid.,* 24.

[59] Dawson, *Politics of Religion,* 87.

[60] *RSS,* v, 141 no. 650 (20 August 1559).

[61] NLS, Crawford Muniments, 3/1/6.

Table 3.1

Campbell Connections

Argyll

Archibald 2nd Earl of Argyll m. Elizabeth Stewart

Colin 3rd Earl

as well as 8 daughters and 3 sons including Katherine's father and her uncle Donald
(all of the above would have been Katherine's uncles and aunts)

Archibald 4th Earl (d. 1558)

Archibald 5th Earl (d. 1573)

Archibald fifth earl of Argyll was Katherine Campbell's second cousin.

Campbell of Cawdor
(Katherine Campbell's parents and siblings)

John Campbell m. Muriel, heiress of Cawdor
(third son of the 2nd earl of Argyll)

Elizabeth
(Possibly Isabel Marjorie)   Margaret   Janet   Katherine : Archibald (d. 1551)   John   Donald   Duncan
                                                              Alexander (Possibly William)

John (d. 1592)

34

3

THE DOWAGER COUNTESS OF CRAWFORD AND THE CAMPBELLS

Within a year of the death of the ninth earl of Crawford in 1558, the religious Reformation had begun to sweep across Scotland with full force. Iconoclasm at Perth following a sermon there by John Knox had empowered the Lords of the Congregation (Scotland's leading Protestants) to pursue their cause openly. Their call for religious reform quickly came to include a political dimension in their demand for the removal of French money and influence (especially religious) from the affairs of Scotland. A new paradigm was offered by the earl of Argyll and others who engineered a diplomatic revolution which drew Scotland away from the traditional French alliance and into a working 'British' relationship with England and the rest of the 'Atlantic archipelago'.[1]

The widowed countess of Crawford may have become a Lindsay by marriage, but she remained a Campbell by birth and affinity and on the death of her second husband she fell under the supervision of her superior male kinsman, the earl of Argyll. As was noted in the introduction to this work, a widow had considerably more freedom of action in society than did her married or unmarried female peers. Putting aside the personal loss which may have been emotionally costly, widowhood could be a liberating and desirable state for a sixteenth-century Scottish woman, particularly for one with sources of income and means of support. The dowager countess of Crawford, as her late husband's executrix, custodian of their children and a woman of means, could exercise considerable independence although this never precluded her obligation to follow the dictates of her clan chief.[1]

That Katherine Campbell was not required to re-marry for a second time, either immediately or later, was probably important, though one can only speculate about why she remained a widow from 1558 until her death in 1578. The fifth earl of Argyll gave ample evidence of his using Campbell widows to further his designs in Ulster and elsewhere. His stepmother Katherine MacLean, widow of the fourth earl, was married to Calvagh O'Donnell in 1560 as part of the fifth earl's overall 'British' strategy. Seven years later he engaged in extensive negotiations to complete the marriages of his aunt Agnes, Lady Kintyre, and of her daughter to Turlough Luinach O'Neill of Ulster and to Hugh O'Donnell respectively, marriages that subsequently 'altered the complexion of politics in Northern Ireland'.[2] Yet Katherine was exempted from these policies. It was rumoured once, in 1565, that the earl was considering another marriage for her, though not in connection with his Irish policies. The English ambassador Thomas Randolph noted in a dispatch that the earl of Cassillis was being considered as a suitable partner for the wealthy widow but nothing seems to have come of the idea, one that the ambassador considered to be the 'greatest marriage in Scotland'.[3] Perhaps his story may have come to him only through gossip rather than fact.

It seems highly probable that Katherine's position in Angus was so dominant that she best served the Campbell interests there as dowager countess of Crawford. Another marriage would have deprived her of the freedom a widow possessed to manage her own affairs and those of her seven younger Lindsay children and her two Ogilvy daughters. Had she remarried she would have had to forfeit her role as tutrix testamentary to her children thus losing both power and influence, while her terce lands would have come under the control of her new husband.[4] In the long run, it would seem, Katherine was most helpful to Campbell interests as an independent widow.[5]

Katherine may have been of use to the earl in another capacity as well. As one of the leading Lords of the Congregation, Argyll was strongly committed to the protestantisation of Scotland. Dundee, Angus and the Mearns, where the Ogilvy and Lindsay influence was widespread, were regions of Scotland where Protestant ideas had taken root and where local lairds and townspeople had adopted the new religion with zeal and commitment. Katherine had numerous ties to many of the Protestant activists (as had her late husband). Amongst the most prominent was John, fifth Lord Erskine, her uncle by marriage, he having married her father's (and Donald Campbell's) sister. The sixth Lord Erskine, who was Katherine's cousin, was an active Lord of the Congregation along with the earl of Argyll.[6] Another close friend to Katherine and her late husband, John Erskine of Dun, was influential in and around Montrose and Brechin where he had hosted visits from George Wishart and John Knox years before the Reformation began in earnest. Dun became superintendent of Angus when the new kirk came into being. His grandson John, fiar of Dun, later became the husband of Agnes Ogilvy, Katherine's daughter.[7] And there were others. William Durham of Grange, yet another staunch Protestant, was one of the curators of David Lindsay of Glenesk as well as being one of Katherine's close associates. The lairds of Inverquharity were drawn into her circle by the marriage of her daughter Helen Ogilvy to the 'young laird'.

Additionally, Katherine's sister's marriage to John Forbes of Towie and that of her son James Ogilvy to Jean, eldest daughter of William seventh Lord Forbes of Forbes cemented ties with strongly Protestant families. All of these connections may have been useful to the earl of Argyll who was active at the political centre in the early 1560s.[8] Furthermore, so long as Katherine remained as the dowager countess of Crawford, she had a free hand to negotiate marriages and to transact business for her children, to benefit the twin causes of affinity and religion.

Yet another good reason for the earl to leave Katherine in Angus as dowager countess of Crawford was Donald Campbell, one time abbot of Coupar Angus and bishop-postulate of Brechin.[9] He had played an important role in establishing a Campbell presence in the region and he and his niece maintained a close, personal, working relationship. Like Katherine, and despite his clerical status, Donald Campbell fathered a large number of children. These he provided for by feuing the abbey's lands and estates. Not only did his sons and daughters profit from this process, which he began well before 1559, but Katherine and her family, and others of the Campbell kin and affinity were favourably served as feuing was speeded up around 1559/60.[10]

Donald Campbell served as curator to Katherine's sons James Ogilvy and David Lindsay. Although this role may have been one of duty rather than affection, Donald's personal trust and regard for his niece are demonstrated in many of the other interactions he had with her. It will be recalled that it was he who made her the copy of her appointment as custodian and tutrix testamentary to her Ogilvy children back in 1545, (see above p.9). Later she and the earl of Crawford lent him money when he made his bid to win the office of bishop of Brechin.[11] The dowager countess and the ex-abbot made a good team representing Campbell interests in Angus.

Donald Campbell's behaviour in the late 1550s suggests that he anticipated the advent of religious reform and the break-up of church lands in the not-too-distant future. Like many people of his profession and generation he was caught between conflicting loyalties to his church and to his chief; between religious reform from within and religious change based on the English or Continental models. This conflict is exemplified by his seeking preferment in the church in attempting to obtain the bishopric of Brechin when it became vacant in 1558.[12] Had he obtained this appointment it would have improved his clerical status and brought new lands and incomes to sustain his lifestyle and his family. It is doubtful that he would have demonstrated any greater moral restraint than he had done at Coupar, or that he would have shown any profound desire to improve the spiritual health of the diocese.

Tacks and leases of Coupar Angus lands dating from the 1550s suggest that Abbot Campbell was becoming increasingly wary of assault and heresy. Clauses requiring leaseholders to be prepared to defend the abbey from physical attack, to uphold the church and to avoid heresy became commonplace in tacks. In fact, those falling into the latter fault could expect to have their leases revoked.[13] These clauses requiring defence of the abbey could well have been for practical as much as for religious reasons. After all, the abbey itself was the place Donald Campbell had called home for over a quarter of a century. Naturally he would want to defend that home and to prevent its destruction. His accelerated feuing of Coupar Angus lands, especially after 1557, dispersed the property, and at the same time allowed him to raise cash in anticipation of an attack on the monastery.[14] Leases to his sons and to members of his extended family just before the Reformation suggest that keeping the abbey's property within the family outweighed any other considerations.

Temporal and political issues had also to be taken into account by the abbot. His clan chief, the fourth earl of Argyll had been one of the original signatories to the December 1557 bond of the Lords of the Congregation. The ultimate goal of these lords was to achieve a religious Reformation throughout Scotland at all costs. Loyalty to one's chief was not a matter of choice, and when the fifth earl (who succeeded his father in 1558) came personally to Coupar Angus in May 1559 to ask Donald Campbell to support the Congregation and to reform his monastery, the abbot may have had few alternatives but to comply with his chief's wishes.[15] Donald Campbell became one of the first of his station to fall in with and give his support to the Lords of the Congregation.

Events surrounding the actual reform of Coupar Angus abbey were of no direct or personal concern to Katherine in 1559. However, following Donald Campbell's death in December 1562, some of what had happened at the abbey two and a half years earlier had a direct effect on her life. What follows here is a brief account, provided as background for some of Katherine's later legal battles. Sometime before the outbreak of the Reformation, and possibly in response to the likelihood of trouble suggested by the 'Beggars Summons',[16] Donald Campbell consigned the 'geir' of the abbey to Katherine Campbell's care.[17] When iconoclasm broke out at Perth on 11 May 1559 the earl of Argyll went almost immediately to Coupar Angus to prevent the destruction and spoliation of the abbey and its lands, according to the English ambassador Croft.[18] At Coupar Argyll convinced his great uncle to consent to reform the place by destroying all the images, removing altars, discontinuing all Catholic worship and replacing these services with prayers and readings in English. It was further determined that the monks might keep their livings but they were to wear secular clothing.[19] The abbot agreed to all of this as well as to furthering the aims of the Lords of the Congregation by making available the resources of the abbey to their armies and by agreeing to vote for reform in parliaments and other national meetings.[20] In short Donald Campbell became a convert to Protestantism. Meanwhile, the 'geir' of the abbey had been (or was at that time) entrusted to the care of Katherine Campbell, possibly at Edzell.

Throughout the weeks and months of turmoil surrounding the Scottish Reformation Katherine Campbell was probably coping with the loss of her second husband and was busy with her children. Prying her widow's terce from the tenth earl further consumed her energies (see Chapter 4) and she played no discernible role in Campbell affairs until the death of her uncle in December 1562. Donald Campbell was a man of about 70 years when he passed away and in his death Katherine lost a close friend. The gift of the abbey's incomes and profits, though not the commend, fell into the hands of the fifth earl of Argyll.[21] Included in this grant were all the furnishings and goods belonging to the place as well as all the profits and debts of the late abbot. When the tenants delayed in paying their rents to him, the earl sued them and Katherine Campbell for recovery of what was his due.

When they were all put to the horn, Katherine Campbell took umbrage and filed suit against the earl, claiming that she should not be horned since she owed him no rents, duties or other profits out of the abbey.[22] In this action Katherine acknowledged her possession of certain goods but she demanded some proof that she was required to give these items up before she surrendered them to the earl. This proof was enclosed with the Lords' charge to her to deliver the items in her possession and comprised several documents now no longer with the collection; nor is it written into the court's record of the case. These documents, she was assured, had been authenticated by Mr John Row, minister at Perth, lawyer, linguist and former papal diplomat, who would most surely have been qualified to assess their validity.[23] Katherine was required to sign a receipt for the delivery of the papers which must have convinced her that she should hand over the items in her possession. Through her procurator she agreed to surrender to the earl all the items listed on condition that her horning be relaxed.[24] The inventory of the gear to be sent to the earl is engrossed in the court's record and is of considerable interest. It consisted of a large number of objects and vestments associated with the celebration of the mass, including chalices, bells, cruets, copes chasubles and stoles.[25] Katherine was instructed to deliver these things to Argyll, but she was told not to ask for or to expect help with the carriage, it being a busy time for the tenants whose work demanded that they remain in the fields![26]

Katherine's uneasy relationship with the earl continued when she became involved in another lengthy and complex dispute with him over her occupation of the lands of Farnell. Argyll had initially come to control Farnell, one of the most valuable properties belonging to the see of Brechin, when between 1557 and 1565 he had administered the temporalities of the bishopric while it remained vacant. When Argyll took the side of the earl of Moray in opposing the marriage of Queen Mary to Henry Lord Darnley in 1565, the Queen withdrew from him the enjoyment of the gift of the fruits of the abbey of Coupar Angus. At the same time she nominated John Sinclair to the bishopric of Brechin taking the administration of the see out of the earl's hands, and promising to use her influence to get the new bishop to set Farnell and other properties to James Lord Ogilvy.[27]

Meanwhile, in October 1565, Katherine Campbell had taken Farnell in tack, with Argyll's approval, and had purchased all the 'goods on the estate and in the Place' for a substantial sum of money. However, her lease was good only until the presentation of the new bishop which occurred in November of that year. Despite these realities, Katherine remained in Farnell and defended her position against the new bishop throughout the winter of 1565-66. When he died in April she was still in possession.

By that time Moray and Argyll had returned to the Queen's favour and to offset his loss of the incomes from Coupar Abbey, Argyll was compensated by the appointment of one of his kin to the see of Brechin with the 'power to alienate its lands at his own [the new bishop's] discretion'.[28] The appointment of the sixteen-year-old son of Campbell of Ardkinglas as bishop of Brechin ensured that the earl of Argyll had a free hand in managing the temporalities of Brechin in his own interest. Subsequent feu charters issued between 1566 and 1568 'were clearly controlled by Argyll' and directly benefited his family, friends and servants alike.[29]

Farnell naturally came into question. Bishop Sinclair feued it to Argyll who in turn subinfeudated it to his servant and adviser Mr John Hutoun. Katherine, however remained in possession and, refusing to remove from the lands, she was sued by the earl of Argyll.[30] As distinct from the legal arguments three letters dealing with this issue and written by the earl of Argyll to Katherine survive in the Crawford muniments. These suggest a high degree of civility between the earl and his great aunt and a certain amount of patience on the part of the former as he negotiated with his persistent relation. In the first, dated January 1568, Argyll tells 'my lady and aunt' that he is not sure what he will do with the mains of Farnell but that he hopes to come to Edzell shortly where 'such things can be reasoned between us'.[31]

In May of that same year another letter from the earl introduced the bearer, Mr John Hutoun,[32] who was being sent in the earl's stead because the press of business precluded a personal visit by him. Hutoun's mission was to obtain Katherine's 'agreement', but what exactly that was, was in either the hands or in the mouth of the emissary and we are not privy to its contents.[33] A third letter from Argyll in the countess's collection indicated that she had not concurred with the terms of the 'agreement' mentioned above, but instead she had sent the earl a counter-offer. The earl claimed personal inexperience in legal matters, in response to her proposition, but on the advice of his lawyer, he would not sign Katherine's contract. Again we are not privy to its contents though Katherine's activism and initiative in defending her claim are certainly evident.[34]

As on previous occasions, the evidence here is that Katherine Campbell was extremely persistent and that she was not to be bullied by her superiors. She herself was on the front line, staying fully abreast of developments and directly involved in matters of interest to her. She attempted several ploys to try to effect some arrangement with the earl so that the debate was still ongoing in October 1569. She consulted her lawyer, Mr David Borthwick, on the matter who in his reply to her noted that she was ill-treated by her chief and by her son, but he knew of no right or title Katherine had to Farnell so he could not comment. If her claim was legitimate, he said, he would certainly defend her interests.[35]

It would be fascinating to have copies of Katherine's letters to the earl which might indicate more fully her line of argument, but it is none the less interesting that she was arguing her claims and that he, for his part, remained civil. He never admitted nor acknowledged Katherine's alleged interest in Farnell, but he was definite about his designs on the land and conveyed that message consistently. The final extant letter from the earl in the collection concludes on a personal note as Argyll assured Katherine that he would send her the horse that she had requested from him as soon as he had a suitable one available for her.[36] The gift he promised to find for her betokens a kindness between them despite their differences. It would be interesting to know if perhaps the white horse which 'I used to ride' and which she bequeathed to her youngest daughter Margaret Lindsay was the one Katherine got from the earl.[37] Katherine did not win on the issue of Farnell but neither did she lose in the long run. She held out for almost five years before conceding to a claim to which she had had no legal title. The earl ordered her to move out, the warning being read by the officer at Edzell and at the parish church of Farnell as well. In March 1570 he leased the lands of Farnell to James Lord Ogilvy in exchange for a loan and a company of footmen supplied to the earl by Ogilvy.[38] Subsequently, Katherine tacked the teinds of Farnell from her son.[39]

Returning to the events surrounding the death of Donald Campbell there was another protracted battle that Katherine fought with one of her Campbell kin whom she pursued with her characteristic tenacity. The letter requiring that she return the abbey's religious items to Argyll ended with a remark that 'Colyne' has gone to Edinburgh to answer her ladyship's charges.[40] These charges turned into a prolonged legal argument between the countess and Colin Campbell of Crunan, one of Abbot Donald's many illegitimate sons who had received the tack of Crunan from his father in 1545 and that of Inverarity in 1557.[41] Colin had been entrusted with delivering to Katherine the abbot's personal bequest to his niece of a number of rings and coins in a purse that the old man carried about on his person. Colin failed to honour his father's wishes and instead contrived to keep the valuables for himself.[42] Katherine had to be both persistent and patient, for it took her fully four years to wrest the purse from Colin's possession.

She began her effort by filing suit against Colin in the court of session. A decreet in her favour did little to get Colin to deliver the purse, nor could a letter from the earl of Argyll move him to action.[43] Thereafter, Colin was ordered to appear before the sheriffs in Dunkeld Cathedral to answer her charges.[44] That too was of no avail and yet another year went by before a commissary court at Dunkeld passed judgment against him, finding that he had done wrong in keeping and failing to deliver the abbot's gift to Katherine. He was ordered to hand over to her the purse with money and rings in it.[45] This, or some other pressure, eventually induced him to act and Katherine got her bequest in the end. It is made known to us by the fact that in her testament certain gifts to her children and servants were noted to have once belonged to the former abbot.[46]

These matters, Abbot Donald's bequest and the dispute over Farnell, were important issues arising between Katherine and her Campbell kin but there were other members of her family with whom she kept in touch on various levels. Her brothers, William of May and Alexander of Flenes each borrowed money from her at different times and she acted as cautioner to the latter for a very large sum of money he owed.[47] Alexander later caused her considerable grief when he nominated her as his executor, a duty that forced her into a very complicated lawsuit with his many debtors and caused her to be harassed by his tenants.[48] This was one fight that Katherine Campbell relinquished and in 1572 she turned over all her interest in Alexander's estate and in the pending action before the court of session to her nephew, John Campbell of Calder.[49] It was unusual for Katherine to give up a fight, but the years 1571-74 were very full ones in the life of the dowager countess of Crawford as her children began to reach adulthood and to raise some questions about her role as executor of their father's will.[50] She hardly needed another testament to execute, especially with all the claims and counter claims on the estate of the deceased Alexander. Better her nephew handle that and profit therefrom, if any profit were eventually to be forthcoming.

Her sister Margaret, mistress of Towie, suffered a cruel death when her husband was absent and the house of Towie was besieged by Adam Gordon and others in 1571. Margaret and her children were burned alive in the house as part of an ongoing feud between the houses of Forbes and Huntly.[51] Shortly thereafter, Katherine Campbell helped her bereaved brother-in-law and her nephew.[52] She was ever generous to her immediate family with financial assistance. Besides her interactions with the Campbells, Katherine had also to deal with troubles caused by David Lindsay the tenth earl of Crawford who refused her her widow's terce and continued to harass her over his perceived loss of the lands of Edzell. These disputes paralleled those with the Campbells throughout the 1560s and are the subject of the next chapter.

NOTES

[1] Dawson, Politics of Religion, 2-3.

[2] Ibid., 105, 155-65, esp. 163.

[3] Keith, History of the Affairs of Church and State in Scotland, ii, 272.

[4] Coutts, 'Wife and Widow', 176-8.

[5] Harris, English Aristocratic Women, 160 noted 'widowhood was the most powerful stage in [English] aristocratic women's life cycles'.

[6] Dawson, Politics of Religion, 24 n. 52. Recent work on the signatories to the First Band identifies Lord Erskine and not John Erskine of Dun as was commonly held: Ibid.

[7] Bardgett, Scotland Reformed, 124. Copies of the contract dated April 1565 survive in NAS, Erskine of Dun Muniments, GD123/140 and in NLS, The Haigh Inventory, Box E II no. 123.

8   Bardgett, *Scotland Reformed*, 124-5. Jean Forbes, Lord Ogilvy's wife, was, like Katherine Campbell, an accomplished and capable manager. When her husband left Scotland for France in 1570 and on his return was imprisoned, adding up to a total of eight years absence from Airlie, Jean managed all of his affairs: Sanderson, *A Kindly Place?*, 139, 144.

9   Donald was a son of the second earl of Argyll and a brother to Katherine's father, making him her uncle. While the see of Brechin remained vacant (1557-1565) the earl of Argyll managed its temporalities: F. Bardgett, 'Dilapidation of Church Property in Angus after 1560', *IR*, 40 (1989), 4, hereafter cited as 'Angus after 1560'.

10   Cowan, 'The Angus Campbells', 30-31 for his family and feuing of the abbey's lands; Sanderson, *Scottish Rural Society*, 127, 129, 132 for Campbell expansion in the region.

11   NAS, Register of Deeds, RD1/2, fo. 359v.

12   *Rentale*, ii, 107-9. Rogers includes here the text of a letter from Campbell's representative in Rome, Mr John Row, later one of the most active first generation Scottish reformers. According to Mark Dilworth, the pope 'steadfastly refused to promote Donald Campbell ... to the see of Brechin unless he gave up his abbacy': M. Dilworth, 'The Commendator System in Scotland', *IR*, 37 (1986), 66.

13   *Rentale*, ii, 79, 114, 145 as examples.

14   Sanderson, *Scottish Rural Society*, 90. He might also have needed the cash in order to pursue his appointment to the see of Brechin.

15   The Earl of Argyll, 'Two Papers from the Argyll Charter Chest', *SHR*, 21 (1923-24), 142-3.

16   A warning, delivered in January 1559, to friars throughout Scotland to quit the premises at the Whitsun term or face eviction: J. Knox, *History of the Reformation in Scotland*, ed. W. C. Dickinson, 2 vols. (Edinburgh, 1949), ii, 255-6.

17   'Geir' is a somewhat all-inclusive word referring to accoutrements.

18   *CSPS*, i, 213 no. 455.

19   *Rentale*, ii, p. vii.

20   Argyll, 'Two Papers', 142-3.

21   *RSS*, v, 639-40 no. 2229; Dilworth, 'Commendator System', 52-54;

22   NAS, ADCS, CS7/29, fos. 106r-107r.

23   NLS, Crawford Muniments, 3/1/5. Row had been Donald Campbell's agent in Rome when the latter was attempting to win the Bishopric of Brechin: *Rentale*, i, 108-9.

24   Another example of withholding money and ornaments is contained in a suit brought by the commendator of Scone Abbey against the chamberlain in 1566 and cited in Sanderson, *Rural Society*, 27.

25 NAS, ADCS, CS7/29, fo. 107r.

26 NLS, Crawford Muniments, 3/1/5. The bearer of this news was Thomas
    Kennedy of Coiff. He was Donald Campbell's nephew and Katherine's cousin,
    his mother being Donald's sister. He was a witness to some of the Coupar-
    Angus charters and received tack of the kirk of Mathe and other properties. He
    was later known as Thomas Kennedy of Kincreich: *Rentale*, ii, 80, 108, 111, 127,
    173-4, 180.

27 NLS, The Haigh Inventory, Box E II no. 170 consisted of 18 papers relating to
    contracts and legal documents between the countess of Crawford, the earl of
    Argyll and the Bishop of Brechin. A note in the margin states that these are
    currently 'missing'.

28 Bardgett, *Scotland Reformed*, 122.

29 Bardgett, 'Angus after 1560', 5 provides a detailed list of these feus.

30 Three years later she was still being urged to remove!

31 NLS, Crawford Muniments, 3/1/1.

32 Argyll's legal servant: Dawson, *Politics of Religion*, 31 n. 82.

33 NLS, Crawford Muniments, 3/1/2.

34 *Ibid.*, 3/1/3.

35 *Ibid.*, 3/2/1.

36 *Ibid.*, NLS, The Haigh Inventory, Box E II no. 170; see n. 27 above. Perhaps these
    missing papers could have provided Katherine Campbell's line of argument!

37 *Ibid.*, 3/1/16.

38 There is much evidence to support a promise made by Mary Queen of Scots to
    James Lord Ogilvy in 1565 of the estate of Farnell: Bardgett, *Scotland Reformed*,
    131; Bardgett, 'Angus after 1560', 7 where the author notes, 'he [Argyll] was
    under pressure to part with Farnell to the magnate to whom it had been
    promised by Queen Mary'.

39 NLS, Crawford Munimnets, 3/2/8.

40 *Ibid.*, 3/1/5.

41 *Rentale*, ii, 120, 152. Colin was designated 'familiar servant' to the abbot and was
    a frequent witness to charters and tacks issued by his father. His lands out of
    Coupar Abbey included Crunan and Inverarity: *Ibid.*

42 NLS, Crawford Muniments, 3/1/10. The estimated value of the contents of the
    purse was £500.

43 *Ibid.*, 3/1/9.

44 *Ibid.*, 3/1/10. An inventory of the contents of the purse is included in this
    document.

45 *Ibid.*, 3/1/11.

46 *Ibid.*, 3/1/16.

47 NAS, Register of Deeds, RD1/8, fos. 207v, 264v.

48 *Clan Campbell*, v, 223; NAS, ADCS, CS7/31, fos. 227v-228r; CS7/47, fos. 405v-407r; CS7/48, fos. 26r-29r; NLS, The Haigh Inventory, Box E II nos. 121, 125, 163, 176.

49 *Ibid.*, no. 185.

50 *Ibid.*, nos. 210, 216.

51 *Memorials and Transactions in Scotland,* 1569-1573, ed. R. Pitcairn, Bannatyune Club (1836), 212-13; Donaldson, *All the Queen's Men,* 126.

52 NLS, The Haigh Inventory, Box E II nos. 181, 233.

EDZELL CASTLE

Drawn from Nature & on Stone by J. Paterson, Montrose. — Printed by Forrester & Nicham.

Plate 1: Edzell Castle, c.1825 from a lithographic print by James Paterson. © Angus Council, Cultural Services.

Plate 2 & 3: Katherine Campbell's Prayer Book (front and back covers) inscribed a 'Prymer of Salysbury use' printed at Rouen by N. Laroux in 1538. The contemporary binding is Parisian work. By kind permission of the Earl of Crawford and Balcarres.

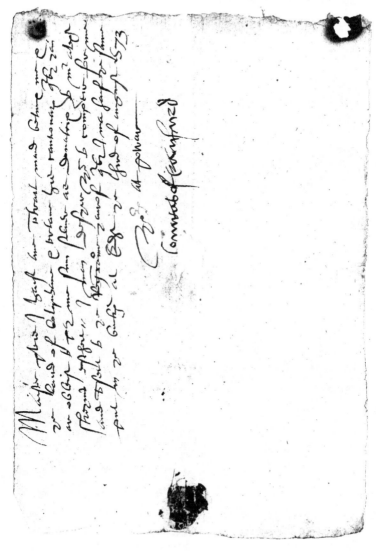

Plate 4: Katherine Campbell signed many of the documents drawn up in her name. Although the signature alone does not imply an ability to write more than one's name, it does suggest that the person could write.

51

Plate 5: Invermark Castle where the ninth earl of Crawford died in 1558. His son, Sir David Lindsay of Edzell, undertook repairs to the castle in the latter part of the sixteenth century. (Photo by the author)

4

THE DOWAGER COUNTESS OF CRAWFORD AND THE LINDSAYS

When Katherine Campbell was widowed for a second time she became the dowager countess of Crawford, but her eldest son had no rights in the earldom and was simply the heir to Edzell. His inheritance, rights and lands came from his father's estate of that name. The tenth earl of Crawford who succeeded to the title in 1558 was Katherine's late husband's adopted son who considered his predecessor as 'frank tenementer of Crawford' and a man who had usurped the title of earl, despite clear evidence to the contrary. Consequently, he showed little concern for his predecessor's widow and her children and he alleged that Katherine had no right to her 'pretended terce ... of the lands and other profits of the earldom'.[1]

Having to fight for her widow's rights was nothing new to Katherine Campbell or others of her status. Katherine had already had first-hand experience when her first husband, the master of Ogilvy, had been killed at Pinkie. His mother and younger brother refused to deliver documents and other rights to Katherine and her son James, causing Katherine to pursue her mother-in-law for the delivery thereof.[2] But, James Ogilvy was heir to Airlie. David Lindsay was not heir to the earldom of Crawford, only to Edzell – yet his mother had rights in the earldom as the dowager countess. It was a much more complex situation. It is noteworthy that Lord Lindsay in his *Lives of the Lindsays* all but omits the tenth earl.[3] Between chapters on the ninth and eleventh earls, he inserts chapters on Lindsays of the Mount and Lindsays of the Byres, and then he continues his narrative with a chapter on the eleventh earl of Crawford. What little he has to say about the tenth earl is engrossed at the end of the chapter on the ninth earl and deals with the former's ungrateful behaviour towards the latter and his family and to the bitter enmity that existed between Crawford and Edzell. Thereafter, the tenth earl is passed over. This was a man with whom Katherine Campbell was forced, by circumstances, to deal repeatedly after she lost her second husband.

The tenth earl of Crawford was but one David Lindsay who provoked Katherine Campbell throughout the 1560s. The others were David Lindsay of Glenesk and David Lindsay of the Haugh of Finavon. The former David was Katherine's eldest (Lindsay) son whose interests she staunchly defended and whose education and marriage she carefully arranged and paid for, only to find him ungrateful and questioning of her administration of his affairs when he reached maturity. Lindsay of the Haugh of Finavon had entered into several agreements with the earl and countess, dating back to 1553, but following the earl's death he failed to honour his commitments causing Katherine a great deal of grief. Throughout the 1560s and into the 1570s Katherine Campbell was kept very busy coping with these three men.

There were other Lindsays in Katherine's life with whom she maintained more compatible relationships. Alexander Lindsay of Vane was a close confidant and supporter as well as curator to at least two of her sons. She placed considerable trust in her late husband's nephew, Mr David Lindsay, as will be shown below. Her younger Lindsay sons, John, Walter, Robert and James were all more generous to their mother than was their elder brother. Clearly, Katherine had friends and allies amongst the Lindsays, but her dealings with all three Davids ranged from troublesome to hostile. Persistence and patience were required on her part, but these were virtues Katherine possessed in full measure. How she handled the enmity of the three Davids will form the central theme of this chapter but some of her more affirmative relationships with other Lindsay family members will perforce find their way into the narrative.

David Lindsay tenth earl of Crawford

David Lindsay, tenth earl of Crawford, was entered into his lands and title following the death of the ninth earl in 1558. He was the son of Alexander, master of Lindsay and Jean Sinclair, a daughter of Henry, third Lord Sinclair. He and his father had been excluded from succeeding to the title because of Alexander's persistent ill will towards his father, the eighth earl. This forfeiture and legal exclusion from succession to the earldom extended to Alexander's descendants, most notably his young son David Lindsay. The 'regulating entail' of 1474, caused the title and lands to pass to the next male heir, David Lindsay of Edzell.[4] Alexander was killed in a brawl in Dundee sometime around 1542-43 though by that time it appeared that the new heir apparent, David Lindsay of Edzell, would not have any children to succeed him. David Lindsay of Edzell consequently adopted and reinstated Alexander's son David as master of Crawford and put him in fee of the earldom.[5] Thus the eighth earl's grandson became tenth earl of Crawford in October 1558 following the death of David Lindsay of Edzell.

There were no challenges to the entry of the tenth earl, but his elevation to the title marked the beginning of a troublesome time for Katherine Campbell who 'inherited his hostility to her [late] husband'.[6] The tenth earl saw no reason to allow her her 'pretended terces' causing her within days of the ninth earl's passing to appear in Forfar sheriff court charging the tenth earl to deliver these to her.[7] As this action dragged on into the following March, Katherine found it impossible to respond to a summons having lately been 'delyvereit of ane barne'.[8] In her stead she sent a sworn procurator to act in her name and shortly thereafter the court ordered the earl to enter the dowager countess to her terce of the earldom of Crawford.[9]

Thus Katherine's primary source of income was confirmed to her, but that did not necessarily guarantee that the tenants would willingly deliver their rents to her. As she soon found out, it became necessary to instigate court actions in order to collect her rents for not only did some not pay, but others went so far as to destroy the crops in the fields so that these could not be sold for rent or profit. Many of these people were, of course, tenants of the earl of Crawford as well, and loyalty to him or instructions from him may have contributed to their malevolence. In either case, Katherine had to resort to the courts to collect her rents or to seize and sell the tenants' goods in lieu thereof. In some cases she obtained letters of removing and in others she sought damages resulting from the intrusions into her lands and the destruction of her crops.[10]

The tenth earl of Crawford may have fallen into line with the court order for acknowledging the legality of Katherine's terce rights but he found other ways to harass her and her children. Perhaps most confrontationally he struck at the house of Edzell by altering the entail of Crawford and obtaining a new charter excluding the Edzell line.[11]

It may have been that the tenth earl strongly resented his predecessor's having excluded the lands and patrimony of Edzell from the earldom but the master and the earl had reached an agreement over Edzell before the latter died.[12] The new earl could not negate its provisions, but that did not necessarily diminish his resentment, and perhaps in retaliation for that perceived injustice, he was determined to alter the entail of the estate to exclude any descendants of the Lindsays of Edzell.[13]

A few months later 'a legal document under the signet of the Queen' noted that the tenth earl was behaving so badly 'that be all law, natural and civil, he deserves disheresing and tinsale [i.e. loss] of the benefit of the said adoption'.[14] His treatment of the dowager countess of Crawford regarding her widow's rights must have been well enough known to have caused this public appraisal of his behaviour towards her, but it did not deter Katherine Campbell. As was the pattern throughout her life, she fought on behalf of her children and their descendants to obtain an annulment of the 1559 alteration. She eventually won the earl's agreement to the re-instatement of Edzell in the entail of Crawford after six years. In March 1565 the 1559 alteration to the entail was annulled as unjust and another was issued restoring the family of Edzell on the failure of male descendants of the tenth earl and others.[15]

Katherine Campbell and her husband David Lindsay of Edzell had spent considerable effort and sums of money acquiring an assortment of rents, lands and miscellaneous incomes with which to endow their younger sons. The tenth earl, using the pretext that these had been acquired by his predecessor, claimed ownership or at least an interest in many of them. Since Katherine held most of the lands and incomes in liferent and heritage, claims raised against her and her sons David and Walter forced her to resort to the courts to protect and defend their rights.[16] Many of these issues were argued over several months and as one was settled another would surface so that throughout the period from 1560 to 1565 Katherine Campbell seemed to be constantly defending her rights against the tenth earl's challenges (or those of his tenants and neighbours) in one place or another.

When, in 1565, the agreement was reached between the dowager countess and the earl over the entail of Edzell, confrontations between the two houses became more muted and less frequent. One gets a sense of just how difficult a person the tenth earl was to deal with from some contemporary comments on his behaviour. In a letter written to Katherine Campbell by her lawyer, Mr David Borthwick, the latter told her that she should not agree to one of the articles in a contract between her and the earl. Borthwick advised the countess that although he wished that she had nothing further to do with the earl, she had best obtain a written agreement from him, not merely his word, despite her having to deal with him further.[17] Borthwick was not the only one to criticise the earl. Alexander Lindsay of Vane complained on one occasion that he was having great difficulty with 'my Lord' who refused to settle an agreement despite Vane's willingness to fulfil its terms.[18]

Besides challenges to her rights by the earl of Crawford, Katherine had to face suits brought against her by others, most contesting her claims to rents or to her rightful possession of certain lands, and others arguing boundary disputes.[19] These she fought and bargained over with her usual tenacity but, on balance, the extant evidence reveals that Katherine Campbell was more frequently the pursuer than the pursued as she sought to collect payments or to defend her own interests as well as those of her sons.

Briefly, two points of clarification should be noted here. In the first place, the dowager countess of Crawford was at liberty to play an active role in all of these matters because she remained a widow. As long as she maintained this special status she was free to act independently. Moreover, her wealth and social status guaranteed that she enjoyed greater freedom in legal and financial affairs.[20] A widow could pursue suits in her own interest. Katherine was obviously aware of the possibility that her status might change at some point and with that in mind she entered into a contract with her nephew Mr David Lindsay, son and heir to her deceased husband's late brother. It was agreed that Mr David would honour Katherine's exercise of the office of tutor to her children as her late husband had willed. If it came to pass that Katherine should 'be mareing hirself' before the children reached maturity, then Mr David agreed to support her should she desire to be renamed tutor dative. Should she fail in her quest to change the appointment, necessitated by another marriage, Katherine agreed to support Mr David's appointment as tutor dative.[21]

In fact, Katherine never had to re-marry, and only once was there a mere rumour of such a possibility when the English ambassador in Edinburgh, Thomas Randolph, wrote to William Cecil in England that he had heard that the richest heiress in Scotland (the dowager countess of Crawford) was being considered for a marriage by her overlord, the earl of Argyll.[22] Randolph's information must have been based on rumour for it remained just that and Katherine continued to act independently and with a widow's freedom until her death in 1578.

Secondly, although Katherine exercised and enjoyed her freedom as a wealthy widow, she relied on the help and expertise of others in her legal and business affairs. Mr David Borthwick, who had served the ninth earl since before Katherine became countess, remained as her legal adviser and representative in Edinburgh and elsewhere. Their few extant letters to one another display a sense of trust and empathy between client and lawyer and when it came time for the countess to send her sons to Paris for their further education Borthwick's son accompanied them and their tutor.[23]

While Borthwick managed Katherine's affairs further afield, she had others closer to home upon whom she could rely as procurators, notaries and trusted advisers. Mr Alexander and Mr Duncan Skene were chief amongst the notaries while Henry Guthrie of Collinstoun appears in many documents relative to her affairs. It was Guthrie who on occasion was the intermediary between the countess in Forfar and her lawyer in Edinburgh.[24] Alexander Lindsay of Vane witnessed numerous documents surrounding her life, was curator to at least two of her sons and seems to have been a constant companion. A servant, Jerome Lindsay ran errands for her all over the countryside.[25]

Katherine relied on all of these people for support and advice but it was she who took the initiative in challenging perceived injustices or demands made of her. Borthwick told her in one letter that he knew of no right or title she had to a piece of property, but if she had some claim he would certainly defend it for her.[26] On another occasion the earl of Argyll wrote to her that he was no expert in the law and would therefore ask his legal adviser to examine her proposal before the contract between them could be signed by him.[27] Katherine Campbell was a lady to be reckoned with. She stood up to her clan chief and to the earl of Crawford. She would do the same with regard to everyone else on down the line to her lowliest tenants and even to the poor soul who lost his life for stealing some of her sheep.[28]

As was noted above, sporadic arguments peppered the relationship between David Lindsay earl of Crawford and the dowager countess in the latter half of the 1560s, but their intensity was diminished or was perhaps overshadowed by greater difficulties that beset the countess in the late 1560s. It seems strange, none the less, that despite the adverse relationship between the two Katherine endeavoured, yet again in the early 1570s, to forge closer ties between the houses of Crawford and Edzell. Her vehicle in this instance was the arrangement of a marriage between her son David and the earl's daughter Helen Lindsay. It has been argued that in promoting this union the dowager hoped to end the hostilities between the two branches of the Lindsay family and certainly the extensive marriage contract and supporting agreements between all the parties would bear out this argument. Repeatedly phrases calling for the cessation of all animosity between the signatories and their heirs, or for love and amity between them, permeate the contracts.[29]

Firstly, there was the contract between David Lindsay, Katherine's son, and his mother in which she gave him the gift of his marriage and he promised to pay her back for all of her expense in purchasing this for him. This is discussed more fully below. The second contract in the marriage series was one between David Lindsay of Glenesk and the earl of Crawford in which it was agreed that the marriage would be settled without any tocher being paid by the bride's father. Instead, Lord Crawford recognized the claims of Edzell to the superiorities of Edzell, Fern, Dalbog and Newdosk (all Edzell lands).[30] Katherine's terce rights in these were confirmed and in a separate agreement between her and the earl, her liferent and her son Walter's heritage in the Haugh of Finavon were confirmed.[31] Following upon all of these was the actual marriage contract which incorporated all of the above agreements as well as others dating back to those made between the eighth earl, Edzell and Helen Lindsay's grandfather, Cardinal Beaton in the early 1540s.[32] Nothing was to be left to chance.

Other agreements between the parties followed over the next three years but, in the main, the Lindsay rift was closed up with the marriage of David of Glenesk to Helen Lindsay. Glenesk, soon to become laird of Edzell and his brother-in-law, the master, soon to be eleventh earl of Crawford, became close companions. The tenth earl died in 1574 and with his passing Katherine was relieved of one of the sources of conflict in her life.

David Lindsay of Glenesk

Katherine Campbell's eldest son from her marriage to the earl of Crawford was known in his youth as David Lindsay of Glenesk. When he became an adult and took up his inheritance he became David Lindsay of Edzell (later Sir David Lindsay of Edzell). This young man cannot have been more than eight years old when his father died. At that time he became heir to Edzell, but it was not until 1573 that he was entered into his inheritance. During the fifteen-year interim, his mother, as tutrix testamentary and custodian to him, as well as to all six other Lindsay children, worked diligently to protect and defend David's lands, rents and incomes. David had four curators in the persons of John earl of Mar (his mother's cousin), James Ogilvy of Airlie (his half brother), William Durham of Grange and Alexander Lindsay of Vane (both close associates of Katherine Campbell in all her affairs).[33] With the exception of the earl of Mar, whose role was probably more honorary than actual, the latter three were in all likelihood, susceptible to the will and wishes of the dowager countess who played an active and dominant role in David's and her other sons' lives throughout their adolescent years. Katherine's responsibility would have been diminished once her children reached the age of curatorship, but she remained a dynamic and interested participant in the guidance of all her sons throughout their youth. It was she who upheld and defended her eldest son's inheritance while he remained a minor and she continued to enhance the family's landholdings by acquiring additional properties for her other sons by purchase, exchange or bequest. She also arranged and paid for their education.

One gets the impression that, like many mothers, Katherine Campbell had troubles with her eldest son as he moved through adolescence and into adulthood. Mr James Lawson, whom she hired as tutor to escort David and his brother John to the University of Paris in 1566, found that although John was a serious student and took advantage of what the schools had to offer him, David was 'not so obedient to my counsall for keping of modestie or [i.e. than] I wuld wiss'.[34] In fact, Lawson went on to say in another communication that David was very willing to be home and that it might be a good idea if his mother were to send for him to return.[35] This she appears to have done, although she did not give up on the idea of further education for him. He and his brothers John and Walter all attended the New College (St Mary's) at the University of St Andrews, with their mother again footing the bill for tuition and board.[36] Although at the time, David may not have valued the education he was receiving, he later became an able administrator and manager of his estates. He kept up a voluminous correspondence, redesigned the garden at Edzell and proposed the building of a new town adjacent to the castle.[37] All of these activities attest to his having made practical use of his education, although these things came to pass later in his life.

From the very earliest days of her widowhood, Katherine had been diligent in protecting David Lindsay's estate and rights. She purchased his relief and marriage in 1559 and she included him for his interest in many of the actions she undertook to collect her rents or to procure receipts for obligations undertaken by her in his name.[38] She obtained a discharge from Queen Mary on behalf of David which relieved him of his late father's obligation to King James V, taken long before David was born.[39] She was nothing if not assiduous in her management of his affairs. By 1571, David was coming close to 20 years of age and arrangements for his marriage were begun. One gets the distinct sense from the extant documentation surrounding the marriage arrangements that there was more to this affair than the simple union of two young people. Some of the details of the many agreements and contracts, between all of the parties involved, which resulted in the marriage of David Lindsay to Helen Lindsay are discussed above. There were further negotiations between mother and son at the same time.

In the first instance, Katherine gave her son the gift of his marriage so that he could 'take to wife whom it shall please him'.[40] If that was the case, why did he choose Helen Lindsay? Was it at his mother's urging or had the two young people perhaps grown up together? (They were married for about twelve years before Helen died, in 1583, and David Lindsay took as his second wife, Isabel Forbes, daughter of Arthur Forbes of Balfour and herself a widow.) Secondly, David Lindsay entered into a contract with his mother whereby he promised to reimburse her for the cost of the gift of his marriage but since he did not have the necessary cash to repay her at the time, a detailed scheme for Katherine's enjoyment of certain lands and incomes was spelled out to ensure his debt to her was paid off.[41] She was also confirmed in her terce lands.[42]

Along with this contract David formally discharged his 'derrest moder' of all her intromissions with his heritage and of the 'great sums of money' paid by her to 'advance me [and my brothers] our houssis and commoditie'. David admitted that he was satisfied with her administration of his affairs during his minority and acknowledged all of her efforts on his behalf, not to mention 'her grete laubouris and traveills tane for the weill relief and mantenance of my house and heretage' as tutrix. Although he was willing to agree to all this and to discharge her of all her intromissions there was one point of contention to which he took exception, namely her handling of the heirship goods entrusted to her.[43] The necessity to record every detail of their arrangements suggests that the relationship between mother and son remained an uneasy one. Although at that time he agreed to withdraw all legal actions he had or might have against her, swearing that he would never bring these up again, as time was to show he did not meet this last condition. Meanwhile, he went along with the marriage.

The marriage contract itself was probably some time in the making and there is evidence to indicate that the countess was an active participant in the negotiations. On the back of her copy of the document Katherine noted 'md [memorandum] To Remember To send mr David Borthwik to aviss with all the contracts e [and] writtings'.[44] Despite all of the good intentions expressed in the marriage arrangements, the ill will between David Lindsay of Glenesk and his mother continued. At his coming of age in June 1573, Katherine handed over to David his castle at Edzell and all its contents. Going from room to room in the castle Katherine compiled an inventory of all the furniture and furnishings from the tables and cupboards in the great hall, to the beds and linens in the various chambers, all the way down to the pots and pans in the kitchen.[45] On the back of this lengthy and most interesting list, a note reveals that on 4 June at six in the evening Dame Katherine offered David Lindsay of Edzell his heirship goods and gear pertaining to his place of Edzell. Both she and the witnesses testified that David refused to receive the goods or to relieve his mother as to do so would be prejudicial to his 'action'.[46]

These heirship goods, the furniture and furnishings of his house, livestock, crops and implements, excepted from his 1571 contract with his mother, became the source of yet another protracted legal battle in which Katherine Campbell was forced to engage. David Lindsay challenged her administration of his late father's testament, claiming that her accounts were inaccurate, that she had unjustly intromitted with certain funds and had defrauded him and his siblings by failing to account for the heirship goods and by undervaluing the crops in the fields and in the barns. He further claimed that she had failed to pay certain of the ninth earl's debts. David Lindsay brought this challenge in name of his siblings, his mother in law and other creditors named in the late earl's testament, but the evidence indicates that he alone (or his procurators) were the only active participants in the proceedings. His motivation for demanding a fuller accounting, oft repeated throughout the proceedings, was that he feared that any inaccuracies or unpaid debts might be charged to him in the future. He was also certain that his mother had not distributed properly the sums of money due to his younger siblings and known as the 'bairns' third'.[47]

Katherine was forced to take up the offensive once again. She raised an action against her eldest son (and the others named) in the commissary court of St Andrews. She set out to prove her just administration with the production of evidence, witnesses and testimonials. The complex and long drawn-out suit was argued principally through procurators for the parties and 'writings' from the principals. Katherine brought in witnesses and evidence to prove her points, including discharges from all of her Lindsay children. Each individually, with consent of curators, or her husband in the case of Elizabeth Lindsay, discharged his/her mother and each declared him/herself satisfied and contented with her expenditures. These included education, the purchase of properties and other financial transactions undertaken by her for the benefit of each. She asked for, and eventually won, exoneration and discharge of the office of executrix and intromissioner of her late husband's estate.[48] The whole process took over two years to come to a conclusion. Besides his mother, David Lindsay also questioned the administration of one of his curators, Alexander Lindsay of Vane.[49] It is perhaps important to note here that Vane was one of Katherine Campbell's closer associates throughout the 1560s and 1570s.

The records indicate that Katherine Campbell had little to do with her son David after 1575. In May of that year he redeemed some of the land he had given her in 1571 as security for the gift of his marriage and two years later he joined his mother in lending money to his uncle and cousin, John and Alexander Forbes of Towie, in exchange for his and his mother's joint infeftment in certain lands of Murthlie.[50] Katherine did not appoint David as one of her executors and although he was remembered in her will, it was only as the eldest son and heir to his father and hardly as a loving son.

Katherine moved from Edzell as her principal place of residence after 1573 and thereafter seemed to be most frequently at the castle of Brechin. In the early 1570s John, Walter and Elizabeth Lindsay came of age and the boys at least offered a complete contrast to their elder brother in their regard for their mother. John Lindsay, later Lord Menmuir, was amply provided for and was always courteous to his mother. His heritage was acquired chiefly through a series of rancour-free dealings between the earl and countess of Crawford, and later the dowager countess, with Mr John Hamilton, abbot of Paisley and later archbishop of St Andrews. Tacks of lands and incomes pertaining to the cathedral at Brechin began the relationship with Hamilton.[51] Incomes from other parishes and church lands were subsequently acquired with presentation to John of the parsonage and vicarage of Lethnot and Lochlee in May 1560. Further lands in the barony of Menmuir followed thereafter and when the holder of the lands and of the parish could no longer cope with the difficulty of collecting rents from his tacksmen, he sold the lands to Dame Katherine and her son John.[52] The bishop of Dunkeld, whose approval was required to ensure John's collation to the parish, imposed one condition on the deal, namely that John be educated at a Catholic university. John subsequently went to Paris to study but also spent time 'at the schools' in Cambridge and closer to home at St Andrews.

One further conflict-free addition to John's heritage was the purchase by his mother of a land, tenement and yard in the Flukargate in Dundee from the earl of Rothes.[53] When John audited and approved his mother's administration of his affairs in 1572, she promised then to infeft him in this property. There was certainly much business to negotiate in the arrangements made for John Lindsay but there was no ill will and no prolonged court actions connected with his inheritance. John did not challenge his mother's management of his affairs, rather he thanked her for her consideration and expense and in lieu of the latter he tacked the teinds of Menmuir to her for three years in 1571 as a means of compensating her for her expenditures.[54] Mr John was collated to Menmuir, Lethnot and Lochlee on 24 June 1574 and three years later he returned to France to continue his studies.[55] Before he left he demonstrated his complete confidence in his mother by leaving her four blank sheets of paper with his signature thereupon so that, should it be necessary, she could conduct his business for him.[56] He gave these to Katherine, rather than to one of his brothers, indicating not only a closeness but also a greater confidence in his mother.

Mr John Lindsay played an active role in shaping Scotland's Kirk and served that institution and its organising bodies in many capacities throughout his career. He also entered the service of the king, became royal secretary and was promoted to the court of session. He was the founder of the estates that formed the original patrimony of the Balcarres family.[57] He did not marry until after his mother had died but his first wife, Marion Guthrie, had numerous ties to the leading Protestants in Edinburgh.[58] Katherine was not so fortunate with the lands and incomes collected to sustain her third son, Walter Lindsay. Maintaining her hold on the Haugh of Finavon, which became the nucleus of Walter's heritage, brought her into prolonged contact and conflict with the third of the David Lindsays referred to above.

David Lindsay of the Haugh of Finavon

Back in the year 1553 David Lindsay of the Haugh of Finavon found himself unable to purchase his inheritance. In exchange for some financial assistance from the earl of Crawford and his wife, David agreed to make the countess and her son assignees in and to the redemption of his lands.[59] In the following year Katherine Campbell benefited further from David's misfortunes when he was forfeited. Katherine also took up his escheat and its associated office of hereditary keeper of the castle of Finavon.[60] Meanwhile, David's mother, Christine Collace, set her terce lands in tack to the countess of Crawford.[61]

David Lindsay of the Haugh found it necessary to borrow more money from the earl and countess who registered this contract in the books of council while shortly thereafter they suspended any reversion promised in this first contract.[62] Following the death of the ninth earl Dame Katherine was confronted by David Lindsay of the Haugh's refusal to remove from her lands at the Haugh of Finavon and she had found it necessary to obtain a court order to force him to do so. His continued obstinate resistance to her attempts to evict him resulted in his denunciation as a rebel by the privy council in 1562.[63] Thereafter Alexander Lindsay of Vane reported to the countess that he had witnessed David and his servants stealing Katherine's corn and taking it 'the back gate way' to be sold.[64]

The decreet for removing was finally executed in July 1564 and Walter Lindsay, Katherine's son, was infeft in the lands of the Haugh of Finavon.[65] Yet a year later Dame Katherine wrote to David Borthwick that she was still being troubled in her possession of the lands of Haugh. David Lindsay continued to interfere with her crops, while at the same time neighbours and tacksmen argued with her about boundaries and old arrangements made with the previous owner or his ancestors.[66] It was a prolonged and acrimonious fight but as was usually the case, Katherine Campbell kept up the pressure and secured the lands of the Haugh of Finavon for her son Walter.[67] As was noted above, she had her rights re-confirmed as part of the agreements surrounding the marriage of her eldest son.

Walter (later Sir Walter of Balgawies) married Margaret Campbell, a sister to David Campbell of Kethick, and possibly a daughter of Donald, late abbot of Coupar Angus. Margaret acquired the feu of the lands of Kemphill and others from the late abbot in December 1550 and brought Walter Lindsay into joint possession of these in August 1571.[68] Walter, like John, was courteous in discharging his mother of her intromissions on his behalf during his minority, but in contrast to John, Walter ended his days as 'one of

Scotland's most noted recusant catholics', zealous and open about his religious choice.[69]

The lands obtained for Robert and James Lindsay were acquired by their mother after the death of her husband and for the most part the provisions were clear-cut and free from dispute.[70] James Lindsay came into half of the west half of the lands of Arnot when his mother called in a debt in 1570.[71] All along Katherine Campbell seems to have been able to capitalise on forfeitures, escheats and non-entries and to have turned these to her advantage. One such purchase became part of the estate of James Lindsay. He received the gift of the ward, nonentry and relief of the 'maid of Lovat'.[72] Mr James became a minister in the Kirk, holding the parsonage of Fettercairn for three years before ill health sent him to the continent in search of a cure.[73] He wrote to his brother John from Paris in 1579, appraising his older sibling of his imminent move to Geneva at the behest of 'writings from the ministry in Scotland', and expressing his trust in John's ability to take care of his interests.[74] He died in Geneva in 1580, leaving as his executor his most Catholic brother, Mr Walter Lindsay![75]

Balhall and Balhalwell were acquired for Robert Lindsay in straightforward sales with only minor disputes over boundaries recorded in 1569 and 1572, the latter being resolved by arbitration.[76] Robert is the most obscure of Katherine's Lindsay sons about whom little is known. Unlike the others, he does not appear to have earned a degree although in his discharge to his mother he acknowledges her expenses on his behalf 'at the schools'.[77] He married and 'lived and died a plain country gentleman'.[78]

Not all of the Lindsays caused Katherine Campbell difficulties, but her relationships with her immediate and extended families were far from conflict-free. There were plenty of issues that occupied and harassed her or which required her attention and initiative. She steadily addressed these. The dowager countess of Crawford must surely have been both literate and numerate. She certainly signed her own name on several extant documents in her archive, but she could hardly have been such a confident negotiator if she had had to rely solely on the assistance of others. Her initiative and use of the courts, her ability to negotiate and to provide instructions to her lawyers, suggests that she was on top of matters affecting her. She kept inventories and accounts and demonstrated foresight and initiative in purchasing lands and incomes. All these activities attest to her business acumen and her intellectual ability.[79] She may indeed have been a bit of a bully at times, but she got things done and was not afraid to stand up to anyone. No doubt this made her some enemies too, but her indomitable spirit and energy were clearly to her advantage and to that of her children.

NOTES

[1] NLS, The Haigh Inventory, Box E no. 174, Box C no. 140; Harris, *English Aristocratic Women*, 134.

[2] NLS, The Haigh Inventory, Box E II nos. 21-23, 25, 27.

[3] Lindsay, *Lives*, i, 201-4.

[4] *Ibid.*, 192, 196. Edzell was a distant cousin of the eighth earl both being descendants of the third earl of Crawford. Edzell and the eighth earl were on particularly good terms: Cameron, *James V*, 106.

[5] Lindsay, *Lives*, i, 194-7. See also ch. 2 above where these events are described in more detail.

[6] Bardgett, *Scotland Reformed*, 124.

[7] NLS, The Haigh Inventory, Box E II nos. 43-49.

[8] *Ibid.*, no. 53. This must have been Margaret, her youngest daughter.

[9] *Ibid.*, no. 54. Instruments of Kenning followed, though somewhat slowly, on 21 April 1559 (Forfarshire) and 3 March 1560 (Perthshire): *ibid.*, nos. 56, 57.

[10] *Ibid.*, no. 73 (poinding), nos. 74, 79, 81, 88 (letters of removing), nos. 80, 82 (destruction of crops).

[11] *RMS*, iv, 300-1 no. 1353 (31 July, 1559).

[12] NLS, Crawford Muniments, 4/1/80.

[13] Lindsay, *Lives*, i, 203-5. Lord Lindsay noted that in July 1559, the queen regent was probably under a certain amount of pressure and she may have given in to the earl because it was advantageous to her at that moment.

[14] *Ibid.*, 202-3, (31 December 1559) citing Haigh Muniment Room. Trouble was often likely to occur when a widow was not the heir's mother: Harris, *English Aristocratic Women*, 135.

[15] Lindsay, *Lives*, i, 203. This charter too was probably politically motivated. It did, however, reactivate the arrangements made between the two houses in 1546 thus 'regulating the entail of 1474': *ibid.*; *RMS*, iv, 371-2 no. 1595; NLS, The

Haigh Inventory, Box C no. 214.

16 *Ibid.*, Box E II nos. 84, 86, 87 (examples).

17 NLS, Crawford Muniments, 3/2/1.

18 NLS, The Haigh Inventory, Box C no. 10 (c. June 1561).

19 *Ibid.*, Box E II nos. 94, 100, 107, 111 as examples; *Clan Campbell,* viii, 37.

20 Sanderson, *A Kindly Place?,* 116; *Women in Scotland,* ed. Ewan and Meikle, esp. chs. 14, 15 and 17.

21 NLS, The Haigh Inventory, Box E II no. 76 (dated 1560, no day); A. Anderson 'Parent and Child' in *An Introduction to Scottish Legal History* (Edinburgh, 1958), 119 noted a mother could be named tutor testamentary but had no right to the office of tutor dative.

22 Lindsay, *Lives,* i, 329; Keith *History of the Affairs of Church and State in Scotland,* ii, 272.

23 NLS, Crawford Muniments, 3/2/12; The Haigh Inventory, Box E II no. 248.

24 NLS, Crawford Muniments, 3/2/1.

25 English aristocratic women had 'dozens' of people who assisted them in every capacity: Harris, *English Aristocratic Women,* 145-52.

26 NLS, Crawford Muniments, 3/2/1.

27 *Ibid.*, 3/1/3.

28 NLS, The Haigh Inventory, Box E II no. 143.

29 Bardgett, *Scotland Reformed,* 135; NLS, Crawford Muniments, 4/1/80; NAS, Register of Deeds, RD1/11, fos. 353r-399v *passim.*

30 NLS, Crawford Muniments, 4/1/80; NAS, Register of Deeds, RD1/11, fos. 384v-395r.

31 NLS, The Haigh Inventory, Box C no. 146; NAS, Register of Deeds, RD1/11, fos. 381r-383v.

32 NLS, Crawford Muniments, 4/1/80. There are numerous other copies of the marriage contract including one in NAS, Regiater of Deeds, RD1/ 11, fos. 384r-395r.

33 NLS, Crawford Muniments, 4/1/82. Donald Campbell served in this capacity until his death.

34 *Ibid.*, 3/2/4.

35 *Ibid.*, 3/2/5.

36 *Ibid.*, 3/1/12, 3/1/13. Receipts signed by Mr John Douglas 'provost of the new college'.

37 *Ibid.*, 4/1/97 (plan), 4/1/1-145, 4/2/1-187, 4/3/1-28, 4/4/1-8, 4/5/1-2 (correspondence and papers). Repairs at the castle of Invermark were also attributed to him: W. Douglas Simpson, 'Invermark Castle', *Proceedings of the Society of Antiquaries,* 68 (Edinburgh, 1933-34), 47; W. Douglas Simpson, *Edzell Castle* (Edinburgh, 1993), 20-24 describes the garden.

[38]   *RSS*, v, 141 no. 650 (18 August 1559); NLS, The Haigh Inventory, Box E II no. 63, Box F nos. 2, 186, 208-13, Box F II no. 1, 2; NAS, ADCS, CS7/21 pt 2 fo. 230r-v for just some examples.

[39]   NLS, The Haigh Inventory, Box F II no. 4. This may have been unnecessary but by securing it Katherine cleared away a problem that might have arisen when David reached maturity.

[40]   NLS, Crawford Muniments, 4/1/82; The Haigh Inventory, Box E II no. 173; NAS, Register of Deeds, RD1/11, fos. 353r-358v.

[41]   *Ibid.*, fos. 358v-362v; NLS, The Haigh Inventory, Box E II no. 174.

[42]   *Ibid.*, nos. 177, 178; NAS, Register of Deeds, RD1/11, fos. 395v-399v.

[43]   NLS, The Haigh Inventory, Box E II no. 174. The discharge was subsequently registered in NAS, Register of Deeds, RD1/11, fos. 358v-362v.

[44]   NLS, Crawford Muniments, 4/1/83. Other drafts and copies of the marriage contract can be found in *ibid.*, 4/1/80, 4/1/81, 4/1/82; The Haigh Inventory, Box F II no. 294, Box C no. 145; NAS, Register of Deeds, RD1/11, fos. 384r-395r.

[45]   NLS, Crawford Muniments, 4/1/84.

[46]   *Ibid.*

[47]   This questioning of a mother's handling of an estate was commonplace in England too: Harris, *English Aristocratic Women,* 136-8.

[48]   NLS, The Haigh Inventory, Box E II no. 210, 1 and 2.

[49]   *Ibid.*, nos. 90, 203.

[50]   *Ibid.*, nos. 215, 233.

[51]   *RMS*, v, 283-5 no. 884. This is a 1585 confirmation of charters dated 1554-57.

[52]   NLS, The Haigh Inventory, Box E II nos. 75, 93, Box F no. 164; Bardgett, *Scotland Reformed,* 125.

[53]   NLS, The Haigh Inventory, Box E II no. 172.

[54]   *Ibid.*, no. 175. Another discharge to her a year later is equally gracious and grateful in its tone: *ibid.*, no. 183.

[55]   *RSS*, vi, 469 no. 2558.

[56]   NLS, The Haigh Inventory, Box E II no. 231.

[57]   Lindsay, *Lives,* i, 334-7.

[58]   Bardgett, *Scotland Reformed,* 151.

[59]   NLS, The Haigh Inventory, Box E no. 247.

[60]   *Ibid.*, Box E II no.36; NAS Register of Deeds, RD1/2, fos. 318v-321r.

[61]   NLS, The Haigh Inventory, Box E II no. 35.

[62]   NAS, Register of Deeds, RD1/2, fo. 399r; NLS, The Haigh Inventory, Box E II no. 40.

[63]   *Ibid.*, Box E II nos. 61, 83; RPC, i, 218.

[64]   NLS, Crawford Muniments, 3/2/6.

65   NLS, The Haigh Inventory, Box E II no. 117.

66   NLS, Crawford Muniments, 3/2/10; The Haigh Inventory, Box E II nos. 145-149.

67   *Ibid.*, Box C no. 146. Confirmation dating from about the time of David Lindsay of Glenesk's marriage.

68   *RMS*, iv, 599 no. 2260. He seems to have been married later in the same year as David Lindsay, ca. 10 June 1574: *Charters of the Abbey of Coupar Angus*, ii, 231, 224; Cowan, 'The Angus Campbells', 31.

69   NLS, The Haigh Inventory, Box E II no. 204; Bardgett, *Scotland Reformed*, 154; Lindsay, *Lives*, i, 327.

70   Harris, *English Aristocratic Women*, 151 noted that investment in land was the 'quintessential mark of successful estate management'.

71   NLS, The Haigh Inventory, Box E II no. 171; *ibid.*, nos. 67 and 85 for her earlier dealings with the laird of Arnot.

72   NLS, Crawford Muniments, 3/1/16.

73   Lindsay, *Lives*, i, 328.

74   *Ibid.*

75   NAS, Register of Testaments, Commissariot of Edinburgh CC8/8/8 fo. 283r; NLS, the Haigh Inventory, Box E II nos. 275-278.

76   NAS, Register of Deeds, RD1/1, fos. 124v-126r; The Haigh Inventory, Box E no. 275; *RMS*, iv, 645 no. 2399; The Haigh Inventory, Box E II nos. 168, 184, 222, 224.

77   *Ibid.*, no. 210.

78   Lindsay, *Lives*, i, 328. There are some bundles of papers relating to Robert in NLS, The Haigh Inventory, Box E II nos. 279-81.

79   NLS, Crawford Muniments, 3/2/9 and 3/2/11 provide just two examples of Katherine receiving reports and sending instructions. NLS, The Haigh Inventory, Box E II no. 198, (an inventory of her rentals in one year); *ibid.*, no. 236 (an inventory of crops destroyed). She utilized both central and local jurisdictions to achieve her purposes. Harris noted that noble English widows learned the necessary legal and estate management skills from working alongside their husbands while the men were alive. Katherine Campbell must have honed her skills in the same way: Harris, *English Aristocratic Women*, 144, 160.

Table 5.1

Lindsay Sons and Daughters

David Lindsay of Edzell   m.   Katherine Campbell
Ninth earl of Crawford

Margaret (d. by 1596)	Elizabeth (d. 1585)	David (d. 1610)	John (d.1596)	Walter (d. 1605)	James (d. 1580)	Robert (d. 1596)
m.	m.	m.	m.	m.		m.
John Lord Innermeath	Patrick Lord Drummond	*Helen Lindsay	*Marion Guthrie	Margaret Campbell		* ? Fullerton
—	—	—	—	—		—
5 sons	2 sons	3 sons	4 sons	1 son		1 son
1 dau.	5 daus.	1 dau.	3 daus.	2 daus.		1 dau.

* David, John and Robert were each married twice, their second marriages occurring long after their mother's death. However, all of their children were born to their first wives.

5

KATHERINE CAMPBELL: RAISING A FAMILY IN POST-REFORMATION SCOTLAND[1]

Throughout the 1560s Katherine Campbell was an extremely busy individual. Her pursuit of the new earl of Crawford for her terce rights and her harassment at the hands of her Lindsay and Campbell kin might have overwhelmed a lesser person, but not the dowager countess. Besides facing those difficulties one must remember that she was left with seven young children all born in the space of about eight years. The five boys and two girls were probably all under ten years old when their father died. In addition to these seven, Katherine had three surviving children from her first marriage, the eldest of whom, a son, had been married in 1558 but he did not reach 'perfect age' until three years later. She also had two Ogilvy daughters who were younger than their brother and were unmarried in 1558.[2]

If being the mother of the heirs to Airlie and to Edzell as well as to eight other children was not enough of a challenge for Katherine Campbell, she had to deal with another dilemma, faced by many of her contemporaries, in that she lived through Scotland's Reformation rebellion of 1559-60. This meant that as her children reached maturity and married in the wake of the religious and political turmoil of the 1560s, they had to make choices about religion and politics which could, and frequently did, divide families.

Although generalisations tend to simplify too much, the overall scene in Angus in the decades prior to the Reformation found the Ogilvies of Airlie (Katherine's first husband's family) as hereditary bailies of Arbroath Abbey, and as such they could be counted as friends of Cardinal David Beaton. They held the same office at the abbey of Coupar-Angus where Katherine's uncle was abbot. These official connections suggest that the Ogilvies of Airlie upheld and supported the traditional religion of Scotland. On the other hand, David Lindsay of Edzell (Katherine's second husband) was a close associate of Sir Thomas Erskine of Brechin, John Erskine of Dun and other favourers of Protestant opinions.[3] Frank Bardgett has shown that social contacts and relationships between the lords and lairds of Angus tended to coalesce along political and religious lines.[4] Hence, living at Airlie in the 1540s and then at Edzell in the 1550s, Katherine was in a position where she witnessed both sides of the political/religious argument just as she was a party to both sides of the Ogilvy/Lindsay feud.

At the Reformation in the years 1559-60, Ogilvy and Lindsay lairds alike 'flocked to the Party of Revolution', but with the return of Queen Mary to her homeland in August 1561, she drew to her side many of those who had supported the revolutionary activism of the religious reformers.[5] It was only after the Queen had abdicated and fled to England that support for her cause came to be associated with the possible restoration of Catholicism and that loyalty to the King's Party meant upholding the recently-established Protestant church.[6] This, however, was in the future and more immediately in 1560 Katherine's chief preoccupation was with protecting her children and raising them to adulthood.

Katherine and all of her children were born in pre-Reformation Scotland and it may be safe to assume that they were all baptised Catholics. All grew to maturity in post-Reformation Scotland. With the exception of James Ogilvy, all were too young in 1559 to show their support for either political or religious factions. As each of these children matured throughout the 1560s and early 1570s, he or she must have been forced to address the issues of loyalty to state and church. These were years during which intense political and religious instability reigned throughout Scotland, and elsewhere, as David and John Lindsay found when they went to Paris with their tutor, and were driven from there by religious friction.[7] This chapter will attempt to assess Katherine Campbell's individual choices in these matters as is evidenced by her very few personal disclosures, and more so by the arrangements she made for the education of her children and for their marriages. The survival of her testamentary papers is a useful tool in this quest as these reveal much about her relationships with her children and about the direction each took as he or she reached adulthood.[8] Firstly, however, let us try to gauge where Katherine herself stood *vis-à-vis* the politics and religion of her life and times.

Katherine's Peers and Associates

When Katherine Campbell came to live at Airlie in the late 1530s, Lutheran teachings were only just beginning to infiltrate Scotland. It is more than likely that she encountered some of the iconoclastic outbursts in Dundee in the summer of 1543 when, following the death of James V, the governor, James Hamilton earl of Arran, briefly adopted a policy of alliance with England and religious reform. Thereafter, Cardinal Beaton won the upper hand in shaping the course of the regency and in staying the demise of Catholicism in Scotland for another decade or more. But the wars surrounding the 'Rough Wooings' persisted throughout the 1540s and most certainly impacted upon Katherine, for at Pinkie in 1547 she lost her first husband. Thereafter, the continued English occupation of Broughty Castle on the Tay estuary caused the country around about to be 'up in arms'.[9] Her father-in-law met his death as part of a force besieging Broughty Castle in an attempt to drive out the English occupants. At the same time her clan chief and others of her neighbours, most notably Patrick Lord Gray, were consorting with the English.[10] All of this brought Protestant opinions into the heart of the Angus countryside so that by 1550 Protestantism amongst the lairds of Angus 'had achieved a wide base' and 'political opinions associated with religious dissent' were easy to identify.[11]

In 1550 Katherine Campbell moved from Airlie to Edzell. David Lindsay of Edzell, ninth earl of Crawford was acknowledged in 1548 along with other Anglophiles as being worthy of a pension whereby he might further the 'godly purpose' of the English.[12] At about the same time his name became linked with a group of Angus lairds associated with dissent, amongst whom were John Erskine of Dun and John, Lord Innermeath. It has been shown in a preceding chapter that throughout the 1550s the earl's wife Katherine had taken an active part with him in managing family affairs, making it more than likely that she came into contact with these lairds and others known to favour religious reform.

Once she became countess of Crawford, Katherine continued to have contact with the abbot of Coupar Angus. He served as curator to James Ogilvy and that alone would have given her cause to stay in touch with him. He was, however, an elderly man in 1559 and as such he may have found it easier to 'go with the flow' and to comply with his great nephew and clan chief, rather than to oppose him and religious reform as well. Most of his past behaviour indicated that he recognised the inevitability of an eventual reformation of religion. He saw outward compliance to its dictates, when it came, as the best possible route to the safety and security of his person and his place.

Katherine Campbell had frequent contact with her uncle in the 1550s and the two remained close. She and the earl of Crawford lent the abbot money for his quest to obtain the bishopric of Brechin in 1558 and she had no scruples about taking advantage of the feuing of church lands or acquiring parochial incomes throughout the 1550s and 60s.[13] These acquisitions became the basis of her younger sons' inheritances and might easily have been influenced by Donald Campbell's example. Later evidence suggests that Katherine's acquisitions had little to do with concern for upholding the church, new or old and this assessment is supported by the fact that she, along with many others, was outlawed for her failure to pay her share to the collector of thirds of benefices in 1563. For her, sustaining a church and a ministry was not as important as providing a suitable means of support for her sons.[14] Furthermore, family loyalty and unity would have impacted upon her just as it did on her uncle, causing her to go along with her chief and senior male relatives. This was certainly the case with the members of the powerful Hamilton family who frequently put family interest over religion making it difficult 'to fully establish outright commitment to a faith'.[15]

After the death of her second husband, Katherine continued her associations with John Erskine of Dun, John Ogilvy of Inverquharity and others in the Protestant camp to the extent that it could be said of her in 1566 that she 'had succeeded in binding to her as protectors for her heirs in Edzell' a solid coalition of Protestant lords.[16] One wonders too why she came to employ Mr James Lawson as her sons' tutor. Admittedly, he was only a young graduate whose opinions may not have been fully formed when he went to work for her, but his letters to her leave no doubt, even at this early stage in his career, of his being firmly on the Protestant side of the religious divide in the mid-1560s.[17] It has been suggested that Lawson went into her service upon the recommendation of Mr Andrew Simpson, minister of the Kirk and Lawson's former schoolmaster at Perth, but how much Katherine actually knew about Lawson's religious views beforehand is not certain. All of this evidence suggests that if Katherine Campbell was at all influenced by the men in her life, then the majority of those closest to her had joined the Protestant camp in the early 1560s.

James Ogilvy was perhaps the most noticeable exception to this group. James had attended the Reformation Parliament with his curator, and uncle, in August 1560. In that year James was still legally under the guardianship of his curators, thus it is more than likely that he voted as he was instructed to do. Once on his own, Ogilvy became a Queen's man whose 'devotion to Mary Stewart was never in doubt'.[18] He and the tenth earl of Crawford joined Queen Mary at Langside but he failed to persuade his brother-in-law, Inverquharity, to link up with them there.[19] Although he publicly professed his loyalty to the King and subsequently won favour with James VI, Lord Ogilvy's sympathies were always questionable.[20] His support for the Marian party and his subsequent self-imposed exile in France, coupled with his imprisonment on his return to Scotland all added up to his being identified as a suspected person in matters of religion. His mother maintained a relationship with him in business affairs throughout her life, but her testamentary papers reveal her basic distrust of her eldest son.

One document that might be thought to provide information about the depth of Katherine's religious conviction is her testament and latter will, but once again we find only ambivalence. She used neither a strictly Catholic formula, nor an overtly Protestant one in the opening statement. Like her contemporary and neighbour Marion Ogilvy, Katherine Campbell 'commendis my soule to the eternell God and my body to be bureit' in the parish kirk of Dundee or in the kirk at Edzell, whichever is more convenient.[21] Margaret Sanderson claims that this phrase was 'used by the Catholic minority in a period when many wills were prefaced with a clear statement of Protestant belief'.[22] Frank Bardgett, on the other hand, finds this to be a neutral phrase which represented the simple piety of the majority who were 'content to die sustained by a conventional, though protestant, faith'.[23] The preamble to Katherine's latter will may thus best be interpreted as indeterminate regarding her religious choice (if she made one) after 1560.

When one looks for clues as to where Katherine Campbell stood in matters of politics during the 1560s one finds that duty and personal interest perhaps best describe her actions as she tried to fulfil her roles as noblewoman, mother and a Campbell. For example, she hosted Queen Mary at Edzell when the latter made her northern progress in 1562.[24] This demonstrates Katherine's important standing in the neighbourhood. Mary's choice to stop at Edzell may have afforded her an opportunity to speak privately with or to seek the support of an important noblewoman; or the castle may have afforded nothing more than the most comfortable resting place for the royal party. Katherine's hospitality was a courtesy and in no way implies that she favoured the Queen or her policies, it was simply a customary duty that a dowager countess, or any noble person in her position, could not refuse.[25]

A clearer indication of where Katherine may have stood politically is provided in an event which grew out of a letter she received from John Ogilvy of Inverquharity. The laird wanted to borrow money from the countess, but he also asked her to keep him informed of any news of interest to the King's Party.[26] When in July 1568 the earl of Morton was due to attend a court in Kirriemuir he chanced to hear of a plot to ambush him. He consequently remained at Glamis and sent in his stead, as his deputies, the laird of Inverquharity and Scrymgeour of Glasswell. The dowager countess of Crawford, meanwhile, discovered the details of the plan, mooted by the earl of Huntly and the Lords Crawford and Ogilvy, and sent the laird and his colleagues a message warning them of the assassins' proximity and designs. They hastily adjourned the proceedings, sent word to Morton who retired from Glamis to the greater safety of Dundee and then escaped themselves, before Huntly and his men arrived, thus completely foiling the attack.[27] By getting word to the king's men she aided their escape and all that was left to Huntly was to retire to Finavon in the company of the earl of Crawford.[28]

On another occasion the dowager countess dispatched a company of bowmen to pursue Adam Gordon after he attacked and burned Katherine's sister and her children in their home at Towie. The feud between Forbes of Towie and Gordon was personal as well as political and Katherine's involvement probably had more to do with avenging her sister's death than with politics.[29] But her swift and decisive action in sending aid to her sister's husband is indicative of her ability to make and execute decisions, even belligerent ones.[30] There is little other material to indicate any interest on Katherine's part in national politics. She does say in her testament that she once attended the court of Mary of Guise, but here again this was a passing single reference. Katherine's primary interest was definitely in her career as mother, tutrix and custodian to her children and in furthering the welfare of the family.

Besides her preoccupation with defending and managing her own lands and those of her children, the dowager countess of Crawford appears to have lived a normal life. She bought jewellery and other items from Edinburgh merchants; she stewarded her lands and corresponded with friends and family.[31] She lent money, took care of nieces and nephews who lost parents and acted as executor for her brother Alexander Campbell of Flenes. She ensured that her sons received good educations, and she continued to purchase property, to take up leases of teinds and to make investments that would benefit her sons when they reached maturity.[32] These were all commonplace duties in the society in which she lived, but her ability to execute all of them and to deal with all the legal challenges that faced her marks the dowager countess as an exceptional woman who more than adequately fulfilled all of the roles expected of a person of her class.[33] Her religious and political views and activities were not recorded in the same official manner as her court appearances, letters and accounts, leaving the impression, although we can never be sure, that religion and politics were secondary to the interests of family in the life of Katherine Campbell.

As her life drew to a close during the summer of 1578, Katherine began to put together her last will and testament. While this document says little about her belief, it does offer strong evidence of her emotional identification with her children. Those with whom she seems to have been closer were those who married Protestants and who by their actions indicated that they favoured Protestantism. She seems to have shown less emotional empathy towards and to have been less attached to those who perhaps never changed or who reverted to Catholicism.

Katherine's Relationships With Her Daughters

Historically, mothers and daughters enjoyed closer relationships than mothers and their sons, particularly the eldest sons. Mothers played a role in promoting daughters' marriages and were frequently active in protecting their daughters' dowries. As a widow, a mother often bequeathed additional cash gifts to her unmarried daughters to enhance the young woman's 'estate', as did Katherine Campbell.[34] In her work on the letters of the fifth earl of Argyll, his kin and family, Jane Dawson found solid evidence to support the suggestion that Campbell noblewomen 'were central figures in the establishment of marriage alliances'.[35] Katherine Campbell, like her kinswomen and the women of her class took care to find out about the prospective spouses of her daughters so as to ensure the most advantageous and suitable union for the future of both daughter and family, before the finalisation of the marriage contract.[36] As a single parent Katherine probably had a relatively free hand. Had she recognised some disadvantage to her immediate or extended family, she would surely have realised the potential for incompatibility and could have led her daughters, at least, into different marriages. Clearly, she expressed her desire for and sought the advantage of familial peace in the marriage of her son David Lindsay to Helen Lindsay.

Katherine and her Ogilvy daughters seem to have been on excellent terms and she had good working relationships with the families into which each of the girls married. Both were recognizably Protestant in their religious affiliation. Agnes's husband was the grandson of the noted reformer John Erskine of Dun. By the 1560s the elder Dun was Superintendent of Angus and the Mearns and he was active in the emerging new Kirk. It was noted earlier that Dun was an associate of the ninth earl of Crawford and that the friendship between the two families dated back to the days before Katherine came to Edzell. Helen Ogilvy married John Ogilvy, younger, of Inverquharity. This young man was a Protestant and became a loyal King's man despite requests from his kin and neighbours to come to the aid of Queen Mary at Langside. He later faithfully served the Regent Morton.[37] Although these marriages reveal nothing personal of Katherine or her daughter, Inverquharity's Protestantism did not distance him from his mother-in-law who continued an amicable association with his family. The same could be said for Katherine's relations with the family into which her daughter Agnes Ogilvy married. Furthermore, the children of both these unions were remembered by their grandmother in her latter will, and both sons-in-law acknowledged receipt of the money and discharged Katherine's executors.[38]

Elizabeth and Margaret Lindsay were much younger than their half sisters, the former being married in 1572 and the latter not until after the death of her mother. Elizabeth Lindsay's union with Patrick, third Lord Drummond seems to have been one that the young people desired, but not one of which the young man's mother approved.[39] According to a letter sent from Scotland to Lord Burghley on 12 April 1572 a meeting had taken place at Perth to try to persuade the dowager Lady Drummond to deal more liberally with her son 'who has married one of the Countess of Crawford's daughters', and to bring the families into closer friendship.[40] This is an interesting comment on the arrangements and raises questions about whether or not Katherine approved of the union, or if possibly the young couple married without any parental consent, thus causing ill feeling all around.

The late Lord Drummond, Patrick's father, was 'nominally a Queen's man' although he was not active in public affairs in the five or so years before his death.[41] Lady Drummond, the young man's mother, was born Lilias Ruthven, and was a sister to the resolutely Protestant Patrick third Lord Ruthven. It was said of her that it was unlikely that she would have raised her son anything except a Protestant[42] but if indeed he was such, Katherine had much less to do with him or Elizabeth, than she had with her other daughters' Protestant husbands. Perhaps her coldness was due in part to the fact that Patrick Lord Drummond's sister Lilias married David, master and later eleventh earl of Crawford, in 1573. This caused Elizabeth and her husband to be drawn into the circle which included the earl of Crawford and Elizabeth's brother David Lindsay of Edzell, none of whom were Katherine's favourite people.

Margaret Lindsay was Katherine's youngest daughter and the object of much motherly concern. Katherine was clearly anxious about Margaret's marriage. As was frequently the case amongst widows of English noblemen, Katherine was very generous to her young unmarried daughter. In her latter will she left 4,000 merks (£2,666 13s 4d) for her youngest daughter's dowry and a further 2,000 merks (£1,333 13s 4d) worth of free goods before any other division of her estate. She also bequeathed to Margaret an assortment of household items with which the young woman might establish her new home when that time came.[43]

Margaret Lindsay was eventually married to John Master of Innermeath, later sixth Lord Innermeath and earl of Atholl. The contract was dated October 1580.[44] The arrangements were probably made by Margaret's brothers David and/or Mr John, and therefore might have no reflection on Katherine Campbell's wishes or preferences. Innermeath's grandfather aided the English at Broughty in the 1540s and was counted amongst the party of revolution by Donaldson making him one of the Protestant lords. The same source credits the young man's father with being a King's man after 1567.[45] Redcastle, the family's Angus property on Lunan Bay, made them neighbours of the Lindsays and Ogilvies, but Innermeath was not one of Katherine's close associates, as were her Ogilvy daughters' families by marriage.

When Katherine drew up her testament in 1578 she remembered all of her daughters in different ways. Helen Ogilvy received a gold necklace and a black satin gown from her mother. Agnes Ogilvy was the recipient of a gold chain along with enough new black damask from which to fashion a gown. Additionally Agnes became the assignee to a debt of 250 merks (£166 13s 4d) owing to her mother.[46] Helen and Agnes Ogilvy's children were remembered by their grandmother with gifts of money but these are the only grandchildren mentioned in the testament. Elizabeth Lindsay received the same personal gifts as her sisters along with some sheets, blankets and pillows, but there was nothing for her children, if she had any by that date.[47] Elizabeth appears to have been her mother's least favourite daughter. When Katherine drew up the first draft of her testament at Dundee in June 1578, Elizabeth was not even mentioned! The fact that she was completely forgotten in the first version of the testament seems to indicate that Elizabeth held no special place in her mother's heart.[48]

Margaret Lindsay, on the other hand, seems to have been her mother's favourite. Besides the 4,000 merks set aside for her marriage and the 2,000 merks over and above, Margaret Lindsay got not one but three dresses, several items of jewellery including necklaces, engraved rings, gold bracelets and her mother's second-best belt chain of gold. Furthermore, Margaret was the recipient of a white horse, which the countess herself used to ride, complete with the best saddle and other tack.[49] Katherine returned to Margaret three or four times throughout the narration of her intentions for the settlement following her death. The fact that Margaret was not married probably warranted this concern. Not only was David Lindsay told to take care of his sister but Margaret was also recommended to the care of Katherine's sister, Lady Lovat.[50]

Meanwhile, the dowager countess did not slight her late husband's illegitimate daughter Janet Lindsay. In March 1563 a contract of marriage was drawn up between Katherine, Janet and William Marshall, son and heir of the late George Marshall of Auchinmarcy.[51] This marriage may not have been of any religious or political significance, but it is interesting in that the busy mother of ten children had time to protect the interests of and see to arrangements for her late husband's illegitimate child as well.

Katherine Campbell's latter will reveals a kindness towards three of her four daughters, as well as to the 'maid of Lovat', who was her niece, and to Margaret Forbes, 'my sister's daughter'.[52] These inclusions, coupled with the attention to Janet's welfare mentioned above, suggest that female relationships were more rewarding to her than were those with her sons.[53] Personal warmth is particularly absent in her bequests to her eldest sons, though less so in her gifts to some of the younger boys.

Katherine's Relationship with her Sons

Katherine Campbell had six sons. There were the two eldest ones, heirs to Airlie and Edzell respectively, along with four brothers of the latter. Her testamentary papers indicate a latent distrust of both her eldest sons, neither of whom she appointed as an executor and a seeming preference for the two sons who served the new Kirk. She appointed all four of the younger sons as her executors.

James, fifth Lord Ogilvy, was remembered in gifts befitting his heritage: silverware and tapestries belonging to his mother from her days at Airlie. David Lindsay's legacy from his mother was similar to that bequeathed to James Ogilvy: a silver bowl and a great gold chain as well as other items suitable to his status as laird of Edzell. There is no hint of warmth, only the demands of duty in these bequests although it could be argued that as heirs they had already inherited the lion's share of their father's estates. Their mother could compensate her younger sons by being more generous to them. Both Ogilvy and Edzell were told that their receipt of the items she bequeathed to them was dependent upon each one refraining from troubling her executors in any way, and neither one was to raise an action against the other on the basis of the old feud.[54] Disobedience to either of these injunctions would cause her gifts to be revoked and distributed amongst the executors. An expression of distrust is evident in these instructions which were accompanied by a charge to all of her Lindsay children to live in harmony with one another 'to stand in mutuell lufe, content and charitie togiddir' in time coming and to remain obedient to their eldest brother 'as becummis the youngest bruther to the eldest'.[55] As was noted elsewhere, James Ogilvy's religious preference was for Catholicism while David Lindsay served the new Kirk 'in a manner appropriate to his status as a lord of a major barony'.[56]

Mr John Lindsay was actually absent from Scotland in 1578 when his mother drew up her testament, but that did not preclude his being named one of her executors. He was already enjoying the rents and incomes from Menmuir, Lethnot and Lochlee, bestowed on him in liferent by his mother (probably when he came of age in December 1573).[57] Besides the lands and incomes collected for him, Katherine bequeathed to John the house she had bought in Dundee along with its contents, and a silver cup 'as a token of remembrance'.[58] He was the only son, besides the eldest, to receive such a handsome gift from his mother who seems to have approved of John and to have expressed her approval in a personal way. She wanted to be remembered to him and to be remembered by him.

Mr James Lindsay also figured prominently in Katherine's latter will. The latter entered the service of the reformed Kirk as minister at Fettercairn. He was the least healthy of Katherine Campbell's Lindsay sons. Lord Lindsay suggests his ailment was 'the stone' for which he eventually went abroad (shortly after Katherine's death) to find a cure.[59] Before his departure he drew up his testament, nominating his brother Walter as his executor.[60] He wrote to John in August 1579 giving news of his forthcoming move to Geneva at the request of the ministry in Scotland and at the same time conveying his confidence in John's ability to take care of his affairs in his absence.[61] He died in Geneva in June 1580. At the time of her death Katherine Campbell owed her son James 1,600 merks (£1,066 13s 4d) she had borrowed from him. She made it clear that this debt was to be honoured before all others and the sum was not to be accounted for by any other profits that might come to him from other bequests. Mr James also received the gift of the ward, nonentry and relief of the 'maid of Lovat' and all the profits pertaining thereto. Katherine had purchased this gift which was to pass to James without division.[62]

While John and James chose to adopt the new religion, Walter Lindsay followed in the footsteps of James Ogilvy and remained attached to the Catholic faith.[63] He had been the beneficiary of much parental generosity since his youth and was a man of substantial property at the time of his mother's death. Although named as one of his mother's executors his only gift from her was a discharge of all the debts he owed to her. These remain unspecified and may have been substantial, but there are no personal gifts to Walter or his children, he is simply dismissed by his mother by her discharge to him.[64]

As a younger son Robert Lindsay is unlikely to have had any practical experience with Catholic practices. He became a partisan of the earl of Crawford and of his eldest brother David Lindsay and was eventually the victim of a fight. Like Walter, he received little from his mother other than the lands and incomes she had procured for him already, though she did specify that all the furnishings and sources of income from his lands were to be his without division amongst his siblings.[65]

Do these indications of her relationships with her surviving children suggest that Katherine Campbell favoured her daughters more than her sons? Do they suggest approval of her daughters' Protestant connections and disapproval of her son James' latent Catholicism or David's volatility? The following table attempts to summarise the relationships just discussed. There are few, if any, consistent patterns which emerge from it.

Table 5.2
Marriages and Allegiances of Katherine Campbell's Children

Katherine's Children	Spouse	Spouse Family	Suggested religion		Allegiance (Males)	
			Cath.	Prot.	King	Queen
James Ogilvy	Jean Forbes (1)	Forbes	James	Jean		X
David Lindsay	Helen Lindsay	Crawford	David?			X
John Lindsay	Marion Guthrie (1)			John Marion	X	
Walter Lindsay	Margaret Campbell	Campbell of Kethic	Walter			X?
James Lindsay	N/A	N/A		James	X?	
Robert Lindsay	--------- Falconer					
Helen Ogilvy	John Ogilvy	Inverquharity		John	X	
Agnes Ogilvy	John Erskine	Dun		John	X	
Elizabeth Lindsay	Patrick Drummond	Drummond		Patrick	X?	
Margaret Lindsay	John Stewart	Innermeath		John	X	

What Table 5.2 does illustrate very clearly is the state of flux that was representative of the decades immediately following the Scottish Reformation. Some people favoured reform, others eschewed it. Some people supported Queen Mary, others gave their allegiance to her infant son. These were not easy times. The decisions were not easy and as Donaldson so clearly illustrates in *All the Queen's Men* 'convictions could find expression in different loyalties as circumstances changed'.[66] Katherine Campbell's closest associates during the years of her widowhood appear to have been favourers of Protestantism, though not all were hostile to the queen. The children she seems to have favoured most were those whose lives led them to be active Protestants or partners of active Protestants. As for herself, she was probably far too busy running her household and defending her interests to have had time to participate in politics and her religion she seems to have kept to herself. Like any good mother she remembered all of her children, but like most mothers of large families she was more partial to some of her children than to others.[67]

NOTES

[1] Portions of this section were incorporated in a paper read at the Sixteenth-century Studies Conference in Denver, Colorado in October 2001.

[2] Finnie, 'House of Hamilton', *IR*, 36 (1985), 5 found that Hamilton marriages produced an average of nine children, six male, three female. Katherine's ten surviving children match this pattern quite closely.

[3] Bardgett, *Scotland Reformed*, 24-29.

[4] *Ibid.*, esp. ch. 3.

[5] Donaldson, *Queen's Men*, 161, 74-75.

[6] This dilemma was commonplace amongst noble families in Scotland. See for example, Finnie, 'House of Hamilton', *IR*, 36 (1985), 14.

[7] NLS, Crawford Muniments, 3/2/4.

[8] *Ibid.*, 3/1/14-20.

[9] *CSPS*, i, 87 no. 176.

[10] Wilson, *House*, i, 107; *CSPS*, i, 67 no. 142, 87 no. 176. Donald Campbell also participated in these activities a) raising a troop and b) making the abbey available as a meeting place between the English agent and Argyll.

11   Bardgett, *Scotland Reformed*, 26-33, 37.

12   *CSPS*, i, 163, no. 323.

13   NAS, Register of Deeds, RD1/2, ii, fos. 359v-360v; Airlie Muniments, GD16/28/11a (Meikle Forthir), GD16/41/21 (Teinds of Linrathan); RSS, vi, 469 no. 2258 (Parsonages and Vicarages of Lethnot and Lochlee); Bardgett, Scotland Reformed 125 (Parish and Parsonage of Menmuir).

14   Rentale, ii, p. xxxiii, 281; NLS The Haigh Inventory, Box E II nos. 187, 191 for examples of Katherine Campbell's failure to pay her 'thirds'; Finnie, 'House of Hamilton', *IR*, 36 (1985), 17.

15   *Ibid.*, 14.

16   Bardgett, *Scotland Reformed*, 125.

17   NLS, Crawford Muniments, 3/2/4, 3/2/5.

18   Wilson, *House*, i, 124.

19   NAS, Ogilvy of Inverquharity Muniments, GD205/Box 1 no. 9.

20   Wilson, *House*, i, 133.

21   NLS, Crawford Muniments, 3/1/16; NAS, Commissariot of Edinburgh, Register of Testaments, CC8/8/7. Confirmed 2 June 1579.

22   Sanderson, *Mary Stewart's People*, 19.

23   Bardgett, *Scotland Reformed*, 148.

24   *RPC*, i, 218.

25   A room by room inventory of the contents of Edzell castle made in 1573 identifies one of the rooms as the 'Queen's Chamber': NLS Crawford Muniments, 3/1/84. Hospitality in elite households in England is explored in F. Heal, *Hospitality in Early Modern England*, (Oxford, 1990).

26   NLS, Crawford Muniments, 3/2/7; The Haigh Inventory, Box E II no. 252.

27   *CSPS*, ii, 471-2 no. 752. This affair is also discussed in Sanderson, *Mary Stewart's People*, 18 where the author identifies the countess of Crawford as Margaret Beaton, the tenth earl's wife.

28   Bardgett, *Scotland Reformed*, 129 provides a list of King's men in Angus. Inverquharity and Scrymgeour are identified as bailies of the regent Morton.

29   *Ibid.*, 128 where the author notes 'the northern feud between the Forbes and the Gordons was taking its place within the context of the civil war'.

30   A contemporary description of this event is to be found in Richard Bannatyne, *Memorials of Transactions in Scotland*, 212-13. He says the attack on Towie occurred in November 1571. Harris noted 'especially close' relationships between sisters: *English Aristocratic Women*, 128.

31   She owed £900 to an apothecary there at the time of her death: NLS, Crawford Muniments, 3/1/19.

32   *Ibid.*, 3/1/7, 3/1/8 (purchases), 3/2/9 (planting trees), 3/2/4, 3/2/5, 3/2/12 (education); The Haigh Inventory, Box E II nos. 68, 106, (property).

[33] Harris, *English Aristocratic Women*, 125 defines a 'good mother' as one who worked to secure her children's futures economically and politically. Widows acquired the requisite skills to carry out the many responsibilities and duties of family and estate management by working alongside their husbands while the latter were alive: *ibid.* 144.

[34] NLS, Crawford Muniments, 3/1/16; Harris, *English Aristocratic Women*, 169, 171.

[35] *Campbell Letters*, 34.

[36] *Ibid.*, 32 where the author says the both sets of parents took part in formulating and agreeing to the contract. Harris noted that not only were aristocratic mothers 'actively involved' in making arrangements for their daughters' marriages, she also found that the negotiations were frequently 'contentious': *English Aristocratic Women*, 111-12, 46.

[37] NAS, Ogilvy of Inverquharity Muniments, GD205/Box 1 nos. 9, 30. The letter was from David Earl of Crawford and James Lord Ogilvy and was written from Melgund, home of Marion Ogilvy: Sanderson, *Mary Stewart's People*, 26-27.

[38] NLS, Crawford Muniments, 3/1/21, 3/1/22. They were the only grandchildren to be remembered in Katherine's testament and latter will.

[39] He succeeded to the title in 1571: *Scots Peerage*, vii, 47.

[40] *CSPS*, iv, 227 no. 242 (Drury to Burghley).

[41] Donaldson, *Queen's Men*, 98, although he had joined the party of revolution in 1560: *ibid.*, 37.

[42] *Scots Peerage*, vii, 47.

[43] NLS, Crawford Muniments, 3/1/16; Harris, *English Aristocratic Women*, 169-71 who asks, was this also a way to divert wealth from eldest sons?: *ibid.*

[44] NLS, Crawford Muniments, 4/1/140-45.

[45] Donaldson, *Queen's Men*, 37, 164, 129. Margaret herself probably never experienced the practice of Catholicism having been born in March 1559, so religion may have been a less critical issue for her.

[46] NLS, Crawford Muniments, 3/1/16.

[47] Between her marriage in 1572 and her death in 1585 Elizabeth gave birth to seven children. At least one or two of these must have been born before 1578: *Scots Peerage*, vii, 47-8.

[48] NLS, Crawford Muniments, 3/1/14 (first draft), 3/1/16 (final draft), 3/1/19 (confirmed copy).

[49] *Ibid.*, 3/1/16.

[50] *Ibid.*, Margaret Lindsay, like her mother, kept records of her affairs: NLS, Crawford Muniments, 4/1/113, 4/1/115 for just two examples. Helen Ogilvy signed her name to the receipt of the bequest to her child: ibid., 3/1/22.

[51] NLS, The Haigh Inventory, Box E II no. 102.

[52] Katherine's sister Janet's first husband was Alexander 4th Lord Lovat with whom she had one daughter, most likely the 'maid', and three sons: *Scots*

Peerage, v, 527-8. The other niece is more difficult to identify. John Forbes of Towie and Margaret Campbell had three sons but there is no mention of a daughter: *House of Forbes*, ed. Alistair and Henrietta Tayler (Spalding Club, 1937), 439.

53   Harris, *English Aristocratic Women*, 9, 28, 128, 168-9 comments on female networks.

54   NLS, Crawford Muniments, 3/1/16.

55   *Ibid.*, was this Katherine Campbell's image of the ideal family?; Harris, *English Aristocratic Women*, 167.

56   Bardgett, *Scotland Reformed*, 151.

57   *RMS*, vi, 569 no. 2167. She had originally acquired this gift for him in May 1560: *RSS*, iv, 469 no. 2558. Mr John was also known as parson of Menmuir though there is no evidence that he served as a minister of the Kirk: *Fasti Ecclesiae Scoticane*, ed. Hew Scott, 8 vols. (Edinburgh, 1925-1950), viii, 504. He later became a very active member of the Protestant community in Edinburgh: Bardgett, *Scotland Reformed*, 151.

58   The house was purchased in December 1570 from the earl of Rothes: NLS, The Haigh Inventory, Box E II no. 172; NLS, Crawford Muniments, 3/1/16.

59   Lindsay, *Lives*, i, 328.

60   NAS, Commissariot of Edinburgh, Register of Testaments, CC8/8/8 fo. 283.

61   Lindsay, *Lives*, i, 328.

62   NLS, Crawford Muniments, 3/1/16.

63   Lindsay, *Lives*, i, 327.

64   NLS, Crawford Muniments, 3/1/16.

65   *Ibid.*

66   Donaldson, *Queen's Men*, 117; Finnie, 'House of Hamilton', *IR*, 36 (1985), 14-15.

67   Many English widows went out of their way to favour younger sons and daughters at the expense of their eldest sons. These gifts often helped the younger children and their families to achieve greater stability and prosperity: Harris, *English Aristocratic Women*, 169, 174.

7

CONCLUSION

Throughout this story of the life of Katherine Campbell reference has been made to the findings of Barbara Harris whose work *English Aristocratic Women* 1450-1550 examines the upbringing, marriages, families and work of her subjects. Harris concludes that the cumulative experience of the women she studied, their activities, responsibilities and duties coupled with their commitment to their spouses, families and kin, amounted to full time careers for each and every one of them.[1] Although some aristocratic women did indeed pursue formal careers in the royal household, many more were wives, mothers and eventually widows who became competent in all these domestic and familial duties.[2] Aristocratic women were brought up to become wives of men of their class and were taught the requisite skills by their own mothers and other female kin and friends to adequately fulfil the role of wife in all its component parts. Household and estate management alone would require basic literary and numeric proficiency as would arranging suitable marriages for their daughters. Many women grew in ability and experience, learning from their husbands how to handle all sorts of family and estate business including the purchase of property for younger, non-inheriting sons, the acquisition of wardships and the management and sale of crops or the purchase of livestock. Since re-marriage was a 'relatively common experience' most widows also dealt with the business of executing their deceased husbands' testaments.[3] Consequently, Harris concludes, in the course of their lives and through their work 'aristocratic women made crucial contributions to the stability and prosperity of their families'.[4] Theirs were full-time careers.

Anyone who examines the life and work of Katherine Campbell must conclude that, like her English counterparts, she too pursued the career of wife, mother and widow with distinction, spirit and energy. She was skilled in all forms of management and impacted significantly on the lives of all of her children. As she neared the end of her life Katherine Campbell continued to manage her affairs, to run her lands and to supervise her household. After mid-March 1578 there are no more business or legal documents in her collection and during the summer of that year she must have come to the realisation that life was nearing its end.[5] In June 1578, while at Dundee, she drew up the first draft of her last will and testament.[6] About three months later, but not before the testament had undergone the scrutiny of a legal expert who urged certain changes and additions, a final version was delivered up at Brechin on 10 August 1578.[7] She died on or about 1 October.[8] Curiously, Katherine did not express any special desire to be buried next to either of her husbands. Harris found the expression of this desire an indication of the woman's feelings towards her spouse, but in Katherine's case, she sought only expediency requiring that she be buried either at Dundee or at Edzell, whichever was more convenient, when death overtook her. [9]

Katherine Campbell's estate at the time of her death was valued at £7,807 13s 4d after all her debts had been deducted. Her wealth lay in extensive farming operations yielding crops and livestock as well as in coined money. She was owed almost £6,000 in cash and rents in kind by her tenants, kin and friends.[10] Her personal debts included substantial sums of money borrowed from various individuals as well as money she owed to several Edinburgh merchants for merchandise and to her servants for their fees. A number of ministers in and around Edzell were due their fees as well and there were various rents that she had not paid amongst her debts.[11]

This detailed listing of her lands, crops, rents and debts illustrates Katherine Campbell's broad range of responsibilities and her wide circle of personal and professional contacts, a circle which reached out well beyond Forfar and Angus. It also demonstrates the size of her personal household which comprised twenty named servants. These included nine 'gentle' men and women and numerous other household helpers such as a steward, a cook, a baker/brewster, a wardrobe keeper, a tailor and a gardener, plus a number of men and boys whose functions were undefined.

Katherine's latter will was discussed in relation to her children as beneficiaries in the preceding chapter and demonstrates her solicitude for their welfare. In addition there were many others of her relatives and close associates whom she included in her final wishes. Nieces and nephews received sums of money ranging from £200 to £40. Henry Guthrie, her long-time servant, and his daughter were also given money. Special bequests to others who had served her included an engraved ring with a sapphire stone (one mentioned as being part of the collection given to Katherine by Abbot Donald Campbell upon his death)[12] was willed to her notary Mr Alexander Skene while a silver cup, 100 merks (£66 13s 4d) and relief from all his debts to her were the rewards given to John Calder of Asloun for a lifetime of service as curator to James and Robert Lindsay and for numerous other functions performed by him on her behalf. Over and above the fees due to them, several of her servants were gifted additional monies or in the case of some of the female servants, one of their mistress's gowns.[13] Katherine showed consideration and generosity in these bequests to those who had assisted her and served her throughout their lives. Her major charitable gift of 300 merks (£200) to the poor hospital at Dundee was circumscribed by the condition that one poor elderly man 'of my kin' was to be admitted there for care. Nomination was to be made by the laird of Edzell.[14]

Katherine Campbell's sons, James Lord Ogilvy, Sir David Lindsay of Edzell, John Lord Menmuir and Sir Walter Lindsay of Balgawies all served James VI personally and professionally in various capacities, with all but John (d. 1598) surviving into the seventeenth century.[15] Her daughters gained less repute at court, although Margaret Lindsay's marriage to John master of Innermeath resulted in her later becoming countess of Atholl. Only Katherine's two younger Ogilvy sons predeceased their mother, although both James and Elizabeth Lindsay died within ten years of her.

Throughout her life Katherine Campbell took control over her affairs and with the help of lawyers, notaries and faithful servants she successfully managed estates, tenants, irascible kinsfolk and her household. Despite all of her skill, one thing she desired eluded her. Over and over again in contracts and arrangements with her children she repeated her wish that they should live together in harmony with one another and that what had happened before their birth regarding the spoliation of Finavon and Glenesk should never become a cause for animosity between them. Her hope was to bind the Ogilvies, the Lindsays of Edzell and the earls of Crawford into amicable relations.

There were signs of the rift healing when James Ogilvy and the tenth earl of Crawford worked together to rally support for Queen Mary in 1568, though in this instance, Ogilvy's brother-in-law failed to join them in their quest.[16] The marriage of David Lindsay of Edzell to the earl of Crawford's daughter in 1571 was contracted with the expressed condition of love and kindness between the two houses and for the ending of all 'controversies' between them.[17] The discharges Katherine Campbell received from her Lindsay children as they reached maturity each contain a clause in which the individual promised to take no further action nor to make any claim resulting from the spoliation of Finavon and Glenesk, undertaken by the Ogilvies of Airlie against their father in the early 1540s.[18] This same theme is repeated in her testament.[19] All of these efforts failed in the long run. After Katherine was dead, feuding, which was endemic to the society and the times, continued. Ogilvies, Lindsays and Campbells alike fought, argued and mutilated one another over various issues, well into the seventeenth century.[20] These matters were naturally beyond Katherine Campbell's control and although they demonstrate that her attempts at pacification failed, it was certainly not due to her negligence or her irascibility. Her sons and grandsons were products of their age, one in which feud and revenge motivated acts of cruelty and violence amongst kin, families and houses.

We are fortunate in that this 'noble and potent lady' has left us such a gold mine of information pertaining to her activities. This work has only begun to excavate the mine, but what it reveals is that Katherine Campbell was a lady who could and did take charge in matters of law, finance and business management on a par with any person, male or female, in her age. Her femininity led her to eschew the male proclivity for feud and violence and to encourage peace and amity amongst the families to which she was joined by birth and through marriage. No doubt there were others of her class and gender who were equally proficient and whose stories have yet to become known from such collections of papers as those amassed and kept safe by the earls of Crawford over almost four centuries; but from this collection Katherine Campbell is revealed as a capable and influential sixteenth-century woman who fulfilled effectively those roles open to her as a wife, a mother and a noble widow of means. In her 'career' as the custodian of her children and their interests she indeed contributed to the prosperity of her family.

NOTES

[1] Harris, *English Aristocratic Women*, 5.

[2] *Ibid.*, esp. ch 9 where the author discusses careers in the royal household.

[3] *Ibid.*, 70.

[4] *Ibid.*, 174.

[5] NLS, The Haigh Inventory, Box E II no. 235.

[6] NLS, Crawford Muniments, 3/1/14.

[7] *Ibid.*, 3/1/15, 3/1/16; Confirmed in June 1579, ibid., 3/1/19 and registered in NAS, Commissariot of Edinburgh, Register of Testaments, CC8/8/7.

[8] NLS, Crawford Muniments, 3/1/19.

[9] Harris, *English Aristocratic Women*, 75; NLS, Crawford Muniments, 3/1/16.

[10] *Ibid.*, 3/1/19; NAS, Register of Testaments, CC8/8/7. Moveables were not separately listed in sixteenth-century testaments: Sanderson, *Mary Stewart's People*, 18.

[11] NLS, Crawford Muniments, 3/1/16.

[12] *Ibid.*, 3/1/10.

[13] *Ibid*, 3/1/16, 3/1/19. Four of her six gentlemen and all three of the gentlewomen named as her servants who were owed their fees received these additional gifts from their mistress. Two of the gentlewomen were the recipients of the gowns: *ibid.*

[14] *Ibid.*; Bardgett, 'Angus After 1560', 17 discusses the follow-up to this bequest.

[15] Founder of the family of Balcarres and ancestor of the present earl of Crawford: *Scots Peerage*, iii, 29; Lindsay, *Lives*, i, 351-80.

[16] NAS, Ogilvy of Inverquharity Muniments, GD 205/Box 1 no. 9.

[17] NLS, Crawford Muniments, 4/1/81.

[18] Copies of the discharges are to be found in various boxes in the Haigh Inventory and are gathered together in Box E II no. 210.

[19] NLS, Crawford Muniments, 3/1/16.

[20] Cowan, *The Angus Campbells*, offers a very comprehensive description of this ongoing animosity and vengeance; see also Bardgett, *Scotland Reformed*, 153; *RPC*, vii, 143.

BIBLIOGRAPHY

MANUSCRIPT SOURCES

National Archives of Scotland

Acts and Decreets of the Lords of Council and Session, CS7.
The Airlie Muniments, GD16.
Commissary of Edinburgh: Register of Testaments, CC8/8.
Erskine of Dun Muniments, GD123.
Ogilvy of Inverquharity Muniments, GD205.
Register of Deeds, RD1.

National Library of Scotland

Muniments of the Earl of Crawford and Balcarres Accession 9769 including the 'Inventory of Scottish Muniments at Haigh'. (A detailed and comprehensive typescript list undertaken by the NRA(S) in 1920 of a vast collection of Deeds and other material. Box E II houses much material relevant to Katherine Campbell, although papers pertinent to her life can be found in numerous other boxes and bundles as well.)

PRINTED PRIMARY SOURCES

Calendar of State Papers Relating to Scotland and Mary Queen of Scots, ed. J. Bain and others (Edinburgh, 1898-1969).
Clan Campbell letters 1559-1583, ed. J. Dawson, (SHS, 1997).
Charters of the Abbey of Coupar Angus ed. D. Easson, 2 vols. (SHS, 1947).

John Knox, *History of the Reformation in Scotland*, 2 vols., ed. W.C. Dickinson (Edinburgh, 1949).

The Letters of King James V, ed. R. K. Hannay (SHS, 1954).

Memorials and Transactions in Scotland, 1569-1573, ed. R. Pitcairn (Bannatyne Club, 1836).

Lord Lindsay, *Lives of the Lindsays*, 3 vols. (London, 1858).

Miscellany of the Spalding Club, ed. J. Stuart, vol. 4 (Aberdeen, 1849).

The Register of the Great Seal of Scotland, ed. J. Thomson and others, 12 vols. (Edinburgh, 1882–1914).

The Register of the Privy Council of Scotland, ed. J. Hill Burton and D. Masson, 14 vols. (Edinburgh, 1877–1898).

The Register of the Privy Seal of Scotland, ed. M. Livingstone and others, 8 vols. (Edinburgh, 1908–).

Rentale of the Cistercian Abbey of Cupar-Angus, ed. C. Rogers (Grampian Club, 1879).

The Scots Peerage, ed. J. B. Paul, 9 vols. (Edinburgh, 1904–1914).

Fasti Ecclesiae Scoticane, ed. Hew Scott, 8 vols. (Edinburgh, 1925-1950).

SECONDARY SOURCES

Anderson, A., 'Parent and Child' in *An Introduction to Scottish Legal History* (Edinburgh, 1958).

Argyll, Duke of, 'Two Papers from the Argyll Charter Chest', in *The Scottish Historical Review*, 21 (1923-24), 142-3.

Bardgett, F., *Scotland Reformed: The Reformation in Angus and the Mearns* (Edinburgh, 1989).

Bardgett, F., 'Dilapidation of Church Property in Angus after 1560', in *Innes Review*, 40 (1989), 3-23.

Brown, Y. and Ferguson, R., eds., *Twisted Sisters: Crime and Deviance in Scotland Since 1400* (East Linton, 2002).

Cameron, J., *James V: The personal Rule, 1528-1542* (East Linton, 1998).

Coutts, W., 'Wife and Widow: The Evidence of Testaments and Marriage Contracts c. 1600' in *Women in Scotland*, ed., Ewan and Meikle, 176-86.

Cowan, E., 'The Angus Campbells and the origins of the Campbell-Ogilvie Feud', in *Scottish Studies*, 25 (1981), 25-38.

Dawson, J., *The Politics of Religion in the Reign of Mary, Queen of Scots. The Earl of Argyll and the Struggle for Britain and Ireland* (Cambridge, 2002).

Donaldson, G., *All The Queen's Men: Power and Politics in Mary Stewart's Scotland* (London, 1983).

Dilworth, M., 'The Commendator System in Scotland' in *Innes Review*, 37 (1986), 51-67.

Ewan, E. and Meikle, M., eds., Women In Scotland c. 1100 - c. 1750 (East Linton, 1999).

Finlay, J., 'Women and Legal Representation in Early Sixteenth-Century Scotland' in *Women In Scotland*, ed., Ewan and Meikle, 165-75.

Finnie, E., 'The House of Hamilton: Patronage, Politics and the Church in the Reformation Period' in *Innes Review*, 36 (1985), 3-28.

Foggie, J. P., *Renaissance Religion in Urban Scotland: The Dominican Order, 1450-1560* (Leiden, 2003).

Keith, R., *History of the Affairs of Church and State in Scotland*, 2 vols. (Spottiswoode Society, 1844-50).

Harris, B., *English Aristocratic Women 1450-1550: Marriage and Family, Property and Careers* (Oxford, 2002).

Heal, F., *Hospitality in Early Modern England* (Oxford, 1990).

Meikle, M., (forthcoming) *Scotland in the long 16th century*, (Edinbugh, 2007).

Merriman, M., *The Rough Wooings: Mary Queen of Scots 1542-1551* (East Linton, 2000).

Paton, H., *The Clan Campbell*, 8 vols. (Edinburgh, 1913-22).

Reddington-Wilde, R., 'A Woman's Place: Birth Order, Gender and Social Status in Highland Houses' in *Women In Scotland*, ed., Ewan and Meikle, 201-9.

Sanderson, M., *Scottish Rural Society in the Sixteenth Century* (Edinburgh, 1982).

Sanderson, M., *Cardinal of Scotland: David Beaton c. 1494-1546* (Edinburgh, 1986).

Sanderson, M., *Mary Stewart's People. Life in Mary Stewart's Scotland* (Edinburgh, 1987).

Sanderson, M., *A Kindly Place? Life in Sixteenth-Century Scotland* (East Linton, 2002).

Simpson, W. Douglas, *Edzell Castle* Historic Scotland Guide (Revised, 1993).

Simpson, W. Douglas, 'Invermark Castle' in *Proceedings of the Society of Antiquaries, 68* (1933-34), 41-50.

Tayler, A. and H., eds. *The House of Forbes*, (Aberdeen, 1937).

Wilson, W., *The House of Airlie*, 3 vols. (London, 1924).

INDEX

INDEX OF PEOPLE

INDEX OF PLACES

The Abertay Historical Society

Honorary Presidents
Lord Provost of the City of Dundee
Principal of the University of Dundee
Principal of the University of St Andrews

President
Steve Connelly

Vice-President
Frances Grieve

General Secretary
Matthew Jarron
University of Dundee Museum Services, Dundee DD1 4HN
e-mail: museum@dundee.ac.uk

Treasurer
Charlotte Lythe
90 Dundee Road, Broughty Ferry, Dundee DD5 1DW
e-mail: c.lythe1@btinternet.com

Book Editors
Dr W Kenefick & Dr A MacDonald
Department of History, University of Dundee, Dundee DD1 4HN

Sales Secretary
Catherine Smith
SUAT, 55 South Methven Street, Perth PH1 5NX
e-mail: csmith@suat.co.uk

The Society was founded in May 1947 and exists to promote interest
in local history. For further information, please visit our website at
www.abertay.org.uk

Publications of the Abertay Historical Society currently in print

No.28   Enid Gauldie, *One Artful and Ambitious Individual, Alexander Riddoch (1745-1822), (Provost of Dundee 1787-1819).* (1989) ISBN 0 900019 24 7

No.34   Ian McCraw, *The Fairs of Dundee.* (1994) ISBN 0 90019 30 1

No.35   Annette M. Smith, *The Nine Trades of Dundee.* (1995) ISBN 0 900019 31 X

No.37   Michael St John, *The Demands of the People, Dundee Radicalism 1850-1870.* (1997) ISBN 0 900019 33 6

No.38   W.M. Mathew, *Keiller's of Dundee, The Rise of the Marmalade Dynasty 1800-1879.* (1998) ISBN 0 900019 35 2

No.39   Lorraine Walsh, *Patrons, Poverty & profit: Organised Charity in Nineteenth Century Dundee.* (2000) ISBN 0 900019 35 2

No.40   Stewart Howe, *William Low & Co., A Family Business History.* (2000) ISBN 0 900019 36 0

No.41   Ian McCraw, *Victorian Dundee at Worship.* (2002) ISBN 0 900019 37 9

No.42   Andrew Murray Scott, *Dundee's Literary Lives vol 1: Fifteenth to Nineteenth Century.* (2003) ISBN 0 900019 38 7

No 43   Andrew Murray Scott, *Dundee's Literary Lives vol 2: Twentieth Century* (2004) ISBN 0 900019 39 5

No 44   Claire Swan, *Scottish Cowboys and the Dundee Investors*
         (2004) ISBN 0 900019 40 9

No 45   Annette M. Smith, *The Guildry of Dundee: A History of the
         Merchant Guild of Dundee up to the 19th century.* (2005)
         ISBN 0 900019 42 5

All publications may be obtained through booksellers or by post from the Hon Sales Secretary, Abertay Historical Society, SUAT, 55 South Methven Street, Perth, PH1 5NX (e-mail: csmith@suat.co.uk)